What Rea

I am having so much fun reading your book! The humor you've injected into a subject that normally reads rather lofty and dry keeps me entertained while it enlightens. I have an idea for a catchy phrase: Effortless Enlightenment!

—Christy Sappenfield
Jacksonville, Florida

Steve Whiteman has clearly "walked the walk" and amply demonstrates it here. The tone and conversational style of his prose is enticing and user-friendly. Rather than characterizing it as a self-help or how-to book, *Swallowing the Avocado of Enlightenment* felt more like a long conversation and an invitation, with tips for living a more spiritual life. The title is provocative, apt, and in itself serves as the first step in inviting the reader to browse, then curl up in an easy chair and stay awhile.

—Karen M. Peluso
Beaufort, South Carolina

Steve's chapter on the Yogas of the West explains the process of spiritual awakening in the modern world in such a simple and clear manner, that I have yet to see its equal in other books. Now I get it—I don't have to pack my bags, leave my family, and travel to India to reach Enlightenment. I'm already on track.

—Pam Swanwick
Broomfield, Colorado

Although you haven't heard from me in months, you have been on my mind regularly. The ripples from your visit were felt for months and I continue to be grateful for the time we spent together. Reading the book is a welcome and gentle reminder when I seem to be knee deep in experiencing life as a struggle. It has lit a fire within me to take a long look at how I really want to experience life.

—Pam Rolandelli
Fletcher, North Carolina

Steve Whiteman's *Swallowing the Avocado of Enlightenment* is a delightfully funny guidebook with serious insights for exploring the elevation of consciousness.

—The Rev. Dr. Jo Williams,
author of *The Song My Soul Remembers*

I'm really finding the work thought provoking and am taking my time to savor it. The thing that is most striking, especially in the dialogue section, is that Steve's language is so easy to digest. His communication style is so simple, yet he is expressing these very complex ideas...like a wild strawberry, pure and basic, but full of layered messages from the air, earth, sun, water, and soil, striking the senses with intense flavor—sweet, but more than sweet. (That's my chef version.)

In my own experiences when I have felt closest to God (my moments of enlightenment), I've felt acutely aware of our paradoxical nature as humans—the double-edged sword of love, hate, fear, etc. Steve has this really easy way of illustrating this. I have tried at times to share my experience of that and found it a very hard concept to articulate. But again, he expresses this paradox very easily. I think anyone will be able to understand this, even if they haven't had a direct experience of enlightenment.

—Cathryn "Chef C" Matthes
Hilton Head, South Carolina

Steve Whiteman is the real deal. I was astounded by his clarity and insight when I first met him ten years ago, and he's only become more masterful since. I consider him my greatest teacher. *Swallowing the Avocado of Enlightenment* will rattle your cage and possibly set you free.

—Brent Bolton
Portland, Oregon

This remarkable book by Steve Whiteman can only be read as a whole and internalized without separation of the parts. It will settle in, shuffle everything you think you know about reality, then re-emerge as a different whole—enlightenment. And you won't realize it is happening until you *NOTICE*.

(No, Steve, you can't have it [the manuscript] back. It's mine, all mine, and I will keep it under my pillow until I've absorbed every word, and put it to work. I am only human, you know.)

—Frank Jordan, author of *Clearing the Way to a Higher Consciousness* and *Earthmind*

Steve Whiteman takes the essential teachings of enlightened masters throughout history and brings them to one powerful practice—Noticing. *Swallowing the Avocado of Enlightenment* skips the endless explanations and theories and shows readers the way to live in perfection. Through real life experiences, he demonstrates that spirituality is not just for the monk in a monastery, but is available to everyone right now. He has helped me to avoid repeating the deeply engrained social patterns and destructive subconscious habits that kept me from peace and joy, and has given me compassionate advice and encouragement along the way.

—Ken Martin
Oakwood, Georgia

I found Steve Whiteman's simple, practical approach very useful. We all know how much has been written to make religious belief and spiritual experiences overly complex and incomprehensible. Above this mountain of human effort, someone has finally presented a very simple and unifying concept.

Steve Whiteman starts the book in the middle of life, as does the human experience itself. He then unfolds the simple truths of walking the spiritual path and simultaneously living in the natural world, just as it is. Even the design of the information flows like life itself, from the middle. *Swallowing the Avocado of Enlightenment* illustrates beautifully how we are born into an already existing experience and given clues along the way to know where we are on the path. This simple picture of being fully human and living life just as it is intended is the clearest view I have seen in over 50 years of metaphysical studies.

This book is a 'must read' for the novice, beginner and those experienced on their spiritual path.

—John Paul Poling, publisher
Community Connexion Magazine

Swallowing the Avocado of ENLIGHTENMENT

A spiritual guide for the rest of us

STEPHEN WHITEMAN

Trillium Center Press
Clarkesville, Georgia

Trillium Center Press
P.O. Box 1479
Clarkesville, GA 30523
888-617-5638
706-754-2170 FAX

Printed in the United States

First printing, January 2006

ISBN: 0-9767264-0-8

Library of Congress Control Number: 2005908870

"...everything you are doing, all of it, is leading directly to your awakening, directly to perceiving the perfection all around you. You're already on track."

—*Stephen Whiteman*

Acknowledgements

Thank you Jenée Wilde—my partner, student, and dearest love—for your assistance with the editing of this book.

And thank you to all my students who, through our dialogues and amazing meals, offered their questions and confusions to inspire the contents and, ultimately, the structure of this book. Special thanks go to Astrid, Ken, Katherine, Will, Michael, Christy, Lee and Gloria for their dedication and service to the work and play of Trillium Center.

Thanks also to Brent and the gang on Mulberry Avenue for their loving friendship and genuine curiosity. And thanks to our other friends in Portland who were there at the beginning and who remain steadfast supporters despite time and distance.

And thanks to Pam, Ken, Ed, Cody, Karen, Cathryn, Frank, John, Lenny and other early readers and reviewers of the manuscript.

Finally, I send my respectful and loving acknowledgment to all of my teachers.

Contents

Swallowing the Avocado of ENLIGHTENMENT

Foreword

In response to a request for testimonials, I received this letter from a remarkable young man whom I had the pleasure to meet on a visit to Portland a few years ago. Our time together was short, but the impression created was long lasting for both of us.

—S.W.

Hi Steve,

Well, where am I to begin? The book you sent me hit me like a brick wall, like a lightning bolt—so powerful and yet so easy to digest. It makes me realize that the spiritual materialism I had been swimming through was not how I wanted to live.

Lately I have had some intense, other-dimensional experiences that, as you stated, often throw one off track. Now I realize I was investing too much energy trying to recreate those experiences. So instead, I have been letting them go—and a lot of other things, too.

I remember the last time we were together, how much I learned from you. But I still seem to get pulled back into my illusion, and I am sure it will happen again. I have noticed, however, that every time I re-emerge from suffering, it seems to be that much clearer, that much brighter.

Today I went to the bookstore, really not intending to find anything in particular. So there I was walking around, and I noticed a book about computer-created 3-D pictures. You know, the one's you have to stare at all tripped-out in your head before the picture pops out? Well, I was doing that when it dawned on me how perfect this was—seeing reality through the illusion. It is amazing the things that emerge into awareness when we wake up—how our awareness begins to expand.

So needless to say, your work has taken a hold on me again, or rather reality has taken a hold on me again. Thanks for that quick slap in the face, the most loving I could have encountered. The fact that I was reading your book and could put to use instantaneously the techniques you were speaking of has great power. How about that for results!!!

And let me tell you something else as well. You do a superb job of speaking to us in a language we can understand. This makes it easy to read and watch the words fall away as the infinite takes hold. There are too many teachers out there who are using ancient jargons or ideas just too complex for life to become simpler.

In fact, the only problem I could foresee with your book is that people might not be able to finish it because the truth speaks so loud. They may realize half way through the book that, like you said, there is a lot less to do than they thought.

I was going to write you a "blurb," blurb-like and all, and then I realized that this would be too much structure for me; it wouldn't be as authentic. So I hope you are okay with dissecting whatever you like from my babble and using it or, if you prefer, using nothing at all. Whatever you do, take to heart how moved I am by you.

Thank you again and again for reminding us of our perfect selves and allowing us to release the guilt and negativity out of our false expectations. At the very least, you will let the world know it is time to stop denying itself of itself, and let the healing begin. I will always consider you my closest of teachers and consider it my duty to unfold for the benefit of all. Thank you for appreciating all of us.

—Cody Clark
Palo Cedro, California

Part I
Life in the Middle

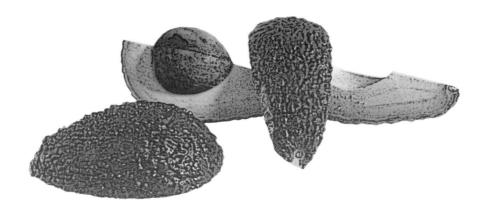

Introduction

From the time you were spit out in this world, your little legs have had to run as fast as they can to catch you up to everything around you—none of which you got to choose. Welcome to the middle.

The middle shows up everywhere. Physically, as far as we can see, feel, and hear in any direction, we're always in the middle. Emotionally, we're always in the middle, caught between parents, siblings, co-workers, children, life goals, and romantic relationships. This is the indeterminable middle—that nagging sense of "Have I arrived yet? Am I where I'm supposed to be? Am I good enough? Am I smart enough? Will I live long enough?"

What comes after the middle? The end of course—enlightenment. When you haven't had an experience of the end, however, you recycle your experience of the middle. This is what it means to be stuck—to have the same experience in different forms over and over again. This is when human life isn't bearing fruit. There's no experience of resolution. The same difficult emotions and life experiences keep appearing over and over again. From my perspective, this accounts for human despair and terminal boredom.

A spiritual experience is when you find yourself out of the middle. This experience of the end—what I call our "natural enlightenment"—provides the only perspective great enough and large enough and true enough to give an immediate accounting of what it is to be human.

Being caught between our confusion and our enlightenment is the dilemma of being Only Human. Is being a human being really a dilemma? Of course not—certainly not from the perspective of enlightenment. But from any other perspective, life can sure feel like all sorts of mischief.

Chapter 1
We're Only Human

Reality presents itself whole all the time. Whole. Already done … ahhhh … and since reality is already complete, there's nothing we *must* do.

Illusion, from my perspective, is what we ordinarily think and feel *about* what's real. Most of what we think and feel comes from a place of separation, where everything seems so clearly to be not whole but fragmented, in process, or incomplete. So we feel there's so much about our selves, our lives, or the world around us that we *must* change. Why is this so? Because human beings are where reality and illusion overlap. We're right in the middle between the direct experience of perfection and our ordinary experience of incompleteness. We're right in the middle, always.

The big green avocado

One day a miracle happens in your life. From God's Tree of Life, one of those really big avocados falls. Your body, recognizing this moment, catapults your arm and hand out and ZAP—you just manage to catch that big green avocado straight from Source. And you get it—this is your chance for enlightenment, and you know what must be done. If you want to stop recycling the middle and wake up in the present forever, all you have to do is swallow the avocado whole. It's just that simple.

But please be honest. Can you swallow it whole? Do you believe that it is even possible? Aren't you pretty sure you'd choke and die if you tried? It's a nice image, a nice idea that waking up would be as simple as swallowing the avocado of enlightenment whole, but in an ordinary way, how can you know beforehand that it is really possible?

So what human beings do is we perceive the avocado and think, "Nope. It can't be done. Wholeness all at once is just too big. Can't I eat it one bite at a time?" Well, no; and yes, you can. So you take the avocado, slice it into wedges, and consume it one piece at a time. This is the task of many, many lifetimes. In fact, this is the task of being Only Human—to take the *somethings* in life and eat them one bite at a time.

This is the strategy, conscious or unconscious, that human beings use everywhere in our lives. We try to perceive life down into manageable bites and bits. We all move from that unimaginable everything to the more apparently obvious somethings. And these somethings fill our lives, don't they? These somethings are the Cheerios and romances and flat tires and bird songs and birthdays and coffee cups and emotions and thoughts and bath towels and promotions and cancers and successes and kitchen sinks that fill our lives. It's the somethings that we try to consume one or two or more bites at a time. This has, in fact, become our way as human beings, and it is very ordinary.

Natural confusion

From life in the middle, all these somethings, all this fragmentation that surrounds us and inhabits our minds, is inherently confusing. Why? Because cultures everywhere demand that we make meaningful connections that our actual experience will refute. We are required to fuse together objects and emotions with the events in our lives to create meaning, even though the meaning will eventually be undone by our actual experience. This is what happens when we grow from toddlers to adolescents, to adults and old age: what we believe to be important is inevitably revealed to be just a temporary belief that for a while binds together emotions and objects and events in our lives in a web of meaning.

You will never lack for meaning; it has a life of its own. If we lived long enough, we would learn not to be seduced by the content of meaning. Instead, we would become fascinated with the process of meaning, its creation and transition. Enlightenment is when the life of meaning is no longer living yours.

How do we begin to undo the web of meaning? By paying attention to your natural confusion. You could say that people's minds resemble a crowded refrigerator door: sticky notes, photos, out-of-date coupons, children's drawings, magnets, stickers. Each item evokes memories and associations about the past and the future. They're usually arranged randomly—some are threatening to fall off, and some are graying and curling at the edges from having been there for so long.

Now imagine that as your eyes scan from item to item on the refrigerator door, each item becomes animated and talks to you. The picture of your old boyfriend waves, and you hear, "Hello, think of me. Why did we part? Don't you still have my Beatles White album?" (which you do). The shopping list says, "More milk! More butter! More chocolate cake (but you know you shouldn't eat it, fatty)!" Soon the sound tracks from the dozens of dancing items on your door overlap and collide. Now everyone else in the kitchen is standing there, mouth open, looking at your refrigerator door. All the items are now three dimensional, many in full color. The picture of your boyfriend is on a little screen with a movie running of scenes from the past and scenarios of what the future might have been. The noise from these clashing conversations is so loud that you can only look at the people in the kitchen and watch their mouths move because you can't hear them!

This would be really strange, wouldn't it? Yet this is happening in people's minds *all the time*. This is confusion, perfectly natural. For those who want to read minds, forget it. It can be pretty overwhelming just to begin to hear and see your own busy mind.

From the time you get up in the morning, everything that you see evokes memories and associations and meaning. Hundreds of conversations are taking place in your head on multiple levels. Some of them you're aware of, but most are still operating completely outside your awareness. And that's just when you got up in the morning. Add to that the rest of your day—the radio station, television, the phone call with your mother, and other random stimulation that requires impromptu responses. In addition, all the objects and people in your life—the chair, the book, the end table that your step-father gave you, your family and friends—provide massive amounts of stimulation to which you must respond, even if most of your responses are outside your awareness. All of this is not a mistake; it's just the way it is, the setup for our natural confusion.

This confusion is what I call being "in the thick of it," like a thick sauce. On a really good day, you may seem to have only a few conversations going on in your head, and the amount of outside stimulation that you have to react to is reduced. The sauce thins enough that you get to see some of the individual ingredients. On a really great day, one memory ends before the next begins; one association pauses and takes a breath before the next association starts. And you get a little bit of space inside and outside. Would it be too soon to say that this spaciousness actually is your mind—that your mind is not just all those random bits and pieces?

What is possible

Remember, reality always comes whole. Only in our feeling and thinking and perceiving can reality be separated into all these somethings—all these pieces that contribute to our natural confusion. Seeing through the illusion of separateness is our path back to Source. This is Source's setup for us, and our way out of the middle.

Rest assured that your life and everything that has ever happened to you is not a mistake. In fact, your life *can't* be a mistake. Your messy life provides the only real motivation for you to change and grow; then awakening is no longer just a nice idea, but an absolute necessity.

Our lives are designed to move from the natural confusion inherent in the middle to an experience of the end, our natural enlightenment. Enlightenment is swallowing the avocado whole—that direct realization of everything all at once. In fact, that's the definition I sometimes use for living in perfection: *the natural, ongoing perception of everything all at once, including yourself.* There's no messing with the somethings, no obsessing with all the pieces that add to our natural confusion. With this, no effort is required to "connect" what is already whole prior to any experience or thought or feeling of separation—*or connection.* You've simply swallowed everything whole.

This is why I refer to all the somethings as illusion, but illusion with a capital "I." Why a capital "I"? Because all these somethings are not a mistake; they are Source's *obvious* path for us to return to living in perfection. How can that be? Because we all begin life in the middle, every one of us, including Buddha, Jesus, and Ramana Maharshi. From living squarely in the middle, we must all begin to transcend the apparent fragmentation and separation. And sooner rather than later, fragmentation will end.

> *Human beings are where reality and illusion overlap.*

But as human beings living in the middle, we're not *just* human beings, you know. We are Only Human. When I say "Only Human," it's both an acknowledgment of our limitations and a celebration of our amazing potential. Say it with me: "I'm *Only Human!*"

The essence of being Only Human is that you find yourself in the middle between the universe's self-demonstration of everything all at once and our perception of all this stuff, all these somethings—right where illusion and reality overlap. Do you doubt this? Consider, has there ever been a time when you were not surrounded by "stuff"? Just look around you. See what I mean? As far as any of you can see and hear in every direction, all the way out into the cosmos, all of us are always in the middle of stuff. Now close your eyes for a few minutes and check inside. What do you find? Just more stuff—thoughts, memories, fantasies. Is all this stuff, both inside and outside of you, a problem? Well, does any of it or any of them or even yourself cause

> *Enlightenment is when the life of meaning is no longer living yours.*

you to suffer? Of course it does. Can you simply toss it all away or ignore it? Have you ever tried? If you have, then you know you can't.

Want to end your suffering? Then don't take all these somethings for granted. They are not a mistake. Your life will not make sense until you return to the actual world. The somethings that make up the actual world are Source's clues left absolutely everywhere, so obvious—perhaps too obvious—and so easily discarded. These clues mark the path back to realization and living in perfection.

•   •   •

Do you have to swallow the avocado of enlightenment whole to become enlightened? Not always. We have discovered another way to become enlightened all at once. You can be turned inside out. Then the stars and planets and comets would be orbiting next to your heart and belly and spleen. Isn't this another way to swallow the universe whole?

Chapter 2
Spiritual Awakening in the West

How can we get out of the experience of the middle? Do we tunnel or blast our way out? Is there an elaborate plan with secret doors and false bottoms? Who will help us? Isn't the middle stacked against us?

From my perspective, *spiritual awakening cannot be avoided*. That's the good news. And though our culture, by and large, does not support spiritual awakenings, the whole structure of life in the middle leads to awakening. More precisely, the very nature of our doing—getting the right career, the right car, the right spouse, the big promotion—leads to incredible stress, which ultimately catapults us into awakening. This doing is our Western yoga.

A long time ago, I decided that anything an individual or a culture experiences over and over again—even though they report that they want it to stop—is worth understanding. To see this, it is important to notice what people *actually* do, not what they *say* they do or *believe* they do. When someone practices something again and again, it becomes a discipline, whether it's meditation, smoking, or overwork.

Like Eastern mystics who rigorously practice to attain control over mind and body, what we actually do in the West—how we live our lives—we do with relentless discipline. And because we're Only Human, sooner rather than later all of this persistent doing will *undo* the illusion of separateness, *undo* our sense of aloneness, and return us to a state of perfection. But few of us do this Western yoga with a willing curiosity. Most of us are what I call "reluctant yogis."

Our three Western yogas

The first yoga is the discipline of doing, or what I call "accomplishment." This yoga shows up in ordinary ways, such as wanting to get a good education, having the right relationship, acquiring lots of stuff, having the right beliefs, hanging out with the right people. This constant search for the "right" way of doing keeps you in the middle because you're only briefly satisfied with all of these accomplishments. From the middle, it seems you're never quite there yet. Everything needs just a little fine-tuning—or a major overhaul.

The yoga of accomplishment even shows up for my friends and students on a spiritual path. They want to have the right spiritual experiences, the right dreams, or know the right truths. Yet sometimes, right in the middle of pursuing spiritual accomplishments, a miracle happens—you catch that avocado without hesitation and swallow it whole. In that infinite moment of enlightenment, you accept everything just the way it is, all at once—and feel satisfied. These moments of spiritual satisfaction, however, get misidentified with what you're thinking or feeling or even doing at the time. So to get more satisfaction, you try to upgrade your thoughts, change your feelings, and find the next better thing to do to reproduce

Spiritual awakening cannot be avoided. That's the good news.

that feeling of satisfaction. But that satisfaction, spiritually speaking, is independent of what you think, feel, or do.

Don't get me wrong; I'm not putting down doing. Does it help to discover your "right" livelihood? Yes. Does it help to let go of negative thinking? Sure. And on your journey to awakening, your thoughts *do* get upgraded, your emotions *do* stabilize and improve. But that's all about the somethings in your life—and getting them right. That's not what the fruit of spiritual work is about.

I hope I don't sound disparaging of accomplishment, because I'm really not. I know that this only-too-human striving for accomplishment has a powerful side effect, which leads us to the second Western yoga—the yoga of stress.

For more than a decade I have carefully observed the yoga of stress at work. Just like athletes who repeat the same motions over and over again to perfect them, we as a culture and as individuals are practicing stress, and we are getting really good at it. For example, consider when our stressful lives interrupt our sleep, so we are awake when we would normally be sleeping. Our worried, whirling minds struggle to answer the Western koans: "Why don't I have more money?" "Why doesn't he/she love me anymore?" "Why me?" "Why this illness?" "Why…." Millions of people, including spiritual seekers, find themselves lying awake in the wee hours of the morning, ripe for a collapse of their ordinary mind, just like yogis everywhere. Are ordinary moms and dads and college students and overworked executives ready for this collapse? Of course not. And so a very real spiritual breakthrough is perceived as a problematic breakdown, and we conclude that life is trying to punish us.

One of my Tibetan teachers once pointed out that in Tibet, even though they live materially impoverished lives, ninety-seven percent of the people are sane and fundamentally happy, and three percent are crazy. In the West, he said, it is reversed. Even though we are materially wealthy compared to Tibet, only three percent of us are sane and ninety-seven percent are crazy. I laughed out loud when he told me this because I knew what he meant. His remark was *not* disparaging; it was simply his direct observation. We *do* live our lives very differently than in his country, and we practice a different yoga to spiritually awaken.

Stress may be a Western form of austerity. In the East, physical austerities such as fasting for weeks and doing tens of thousands of prostrations are sometimes used to stress the body and mind and invoke a spiritual experience. What we do in the West is punish ourselves with the physical and emotional stress of accomplishment. Get the right job, the right mate, the right experiences, enough money, enough recognition, enough love, and so on. Of course, "right" and "enough" never stay in one place for long, so we must keep accomplishing. Whether we are upsizing or downsizing, elaborating or simplifying, this desire to accomplish and "get it right" is at the heart of the yoga of stress, and it is rigorous and unrelenting.

I'm not trying to sell stress; all I'm pointing out is that you've already bought it and are fundamentally committed to it—the stress of accomplishment. Now what do you do? Many books have been written on stress. Some suggest that you should avoid stress; others say stress is unavoidable and you should master it. Most say that our doing in the world produces stress; it's been called an unavoidable by-product of living. In a practical way, all of the above seems to be true. In fact, looking at accomplishment and stress together, it is clear that the more people accomplish, and the more they seek to accomplish, the greater their levels of stress.

A young man spoke to me on the phone the other day and expressed his desire to own a raw food restaurant. He is a very capable person who requires a great deal of himself both in business and his spiritual life. We talked a little about the commitment involved, the demands of his current business, and the stress associated with opening and running a restaurant. He said, "You don't understand, I don't want to operate one restaurant; I want to have a chain of restaurants." He signed up for the graduate course in stress.

Most of us are what I call "reluctant yogis."

Stress also can be a part of spiritual accomplishments, a natural by-product of spiritual growth and maturity. Have no doubt—spiritual practice can be stressful. Spiritual practices are developmental; the arduousness, the complexity, and the number of hours generally increase over time.

Am I disparaging our Western yoga of stress? Well, yes and no, but mostly I am very impressed. One of my teachers would rather do a dark, silent retreat in a cave for a year than do what we do. I'm not kidding. Of course, he would get *lots* of preparation. I do disparage our lack of training or even introduction to our demanding yogas. As far as I can tell, few are aware that our ordinary lives by themselves are a yoga that *will bear fruit*. Lama Rinchen often pointed to "the fruit of the practice," encouraging us not to lose sight of why we are doing a specific practice. That way, when our practice matures and ripens, we can enjoy the fruit and move on. *The fruit of accomplishment and stress is awakening*, our third Western yoga.

For almost everyone, sometime in their lives, often between the ages of twenty-five and forty-five, the yoga that is the "stress" of living will reach a climax—a so-called "mid-life crisis." When this happens, one's life no longer makes sense the way it did; accomplishments no longer hold the same fascination and reward. At this time, it's not uncommon for people to experience insomnia, a life-threatening illness, the end of a long-term relationship, or the end of a career. The result often is severe disorientation: people lose the way they were going, and the path they were on seems to have come to an end. They may have no interest in their current friends. When they look around them, the world of work and accomplishment makes no sense; it has lost its meaning.

During this period of disorientation, which may last months or years, there is often profound disillusionment and an intense seeking—perhaps to return to life as it was, or perhaps to discover a new life. What may follow is a rapid succession of relationships, careers begun and ended, new diets, and other behavior changes. People may also experience unusual thoughts, dreams, fantasies, and desires from earlier in life—even childhood. In general, however, none of these changes brings the relief and satisfaction people are looking for.

In our culture, this would seem to be a period of great suffering—a midlife crisis. But it can also be a time of celebration, because what follows the breaking up of your illusions is the yoga of awakening.

Enjoying the fruit

Stress and accomplishment are what we do, but since we do them without any self-awareness, there's little spiritual joy in doing them. What if we noticed that how we actually live our lives is a powerful, transforming discipline? Wouldn't it make spiritual pursuit and our everyday lives so much easier? How would ambition, including spiritual ambition, feel different? How would we look at it differently? How much more perspective and humor could we bring to our lives if we could anticipate the coming awakening with curiosity rather than dread? It would make all the difference in the world. And our lives could change without the emotional "violence" that accompanies most changes we try to make and the changes that seem to just happen to us.

Culture doesn't help our stress levels. It says you have to do the job interview, go on dates, get married, make a lot of money, and pay your mortgage. When you complete the job interview, you may feel relief and say, "I'm done." But in fact, you're not done. You're still in the middle. Sooner or later, you'll have to go for a promotion or get fired or have some children or find a new lover.

What if our never-ending list of personal and spiritual accomplishments was framed as "this is what we do in this culture to spiritually awaken"? The light bulb would go on. You might learn to notice and accept all that you have to do that you don't really want to do. You might learn to appreciate what all this doing will do *for* you. In my experience, this appreciation is a very real celebration that transforms what had been frightening, depressing, or boring. It transforms the accomplishment and stress into awakening, and in the process you will naturally discover that *there is a lot less to do than you thought.*

What I'm proposing is so practical—and spiritual. As soon as you can, come to realize that accomplishment and stress—as Western yogas—are just as powerful as any spiritual practice done in the East. They will lead you away from endlessly recycling the middle and move you toward an experience of the end—spiritual wakening.

As my three children grew up and left home, I tried to acquaint them with our cultural yogas. I told them, as you make your way through life, you will probably want *a lot of stuff.* You'll have romances, perhaps get married, break someone's heart, get divorced, get sick, make money, lose money, be incredibly happy, be incredibly sad, get lazy, get ambitious, and so on. And then, sometime in the middle of all of this, your life will not make any sense no matter how you try to understand it.

At this point, you're going to have a kind of a breakthrough. It might feel a lot like a breakdown—you might stop sleeping or gain a lot of weight. Who knows what's going to happen. But when it does, give me a call because there probably won't be anybody else in your life who is going to say, "Congratulations!" Not for the suffering, but congratulations on getting to see through so many illusions all at once. If your fortunes are mixed, you may have mystical experiences that accompany this midlife passage. You may hear voices, see visions, and feel unusual body sensations. And though culture may try to convince you otherwise, know that you are not crazy; learn to notice, not medicate.

Why did I tell my teenage children that all this was going to happen? So it won't come as a surprise and won't necessarily bring them to an early grave in the pursuit of more money—*or enlightenment.* Can the pursuit of enlightenment produce stress? Yes! I see it all the time. Yet it doesn't have to be that way.

.   .   .

As a teacher, it is so much fun when a student gets the fundamental setup of our lives, i.e., that our Western lifestyle is not going to radically change soon for most of us, and that's okay, because this life not only can be but is a rigorous spiritual discipline. Are there important differences between a typical Western lifestyle and life in a monastery? Pause before you answer—it's a trick question. Of course there are important differences: no phones, no TV, restricted access to culture, possible celibacy, rigorous practices. Does this sound true to you, or possibly too easy an answer? Let's try "no," there are no important differences. That sounds absurd, doesn't it? Aren't there exactly the differences I just pointed out?

Our Western yogas are as powerful as any spiritual practice done in the East.

The paradox in the question points to how most people create a fundamental split between the secular and the sacred. They believe living a genuinely spiritual life must involve special practices, sacred spaces, or meditative contemplation; feeding their kids and getting them off to school is something different. Enlightenment, without you asking for it, undoes the split. How? From the place of enlightenment, there are no differences that are fundamental between our Western lifestyle and a monastery; it comes back to what it is to be Only Human, whether you're on your way to daycare or to bathe before morning prayers. A common thread that runs through the whole human endeavor is accomplishment. Even monks have an intention, something they're *trying* to accomplish. Many mystics and saints talk of the sheer difficulty of the task and the desire to complete the pursuit, to reach the goal—whether the goal is desirelessness or union with God. From the point of view of anyone *trying*, including trying to give up trying, accomplishment and the stress of accomplishment *cannot be avoided.*

This pursuit and resulting stress is all pre-enlightenment. It's God's setup to lead you back to Source, to awakening. With realization, everything all at once is perceived as being done, complete, in and of itself, including you. From that place, there is an experience of the world *before* it is split into good-bad, right-wrong, sacred-secular, monk-mother. From the enlightenment perspective, everything you are doing, all of it, is leading directly to your awakening, directly to perceiving the perfection all around you. *You're already on track.*

Part II
The Ending

Introduction

It doesn't matter whether what interrupts our clear seeing is frustration, or anger, or jealousy, or the doorbell, or romance, or a brilliant idea, or the baby, or cancer, or the whistle of the teakettle. All of these are the *somethings* that fill our lives.

But in moments of spiritual enlightenment, *everything all at once* is experienced as perfect, including you. Leaving the endless repetition and suffering of the middle, you discover the end. This is the miracle, the experience of it's all done—and it's all perfect, just the way it is. This is waking up one morning and looking at yet another stack of dirty dishes, and through grace or practice, you get it—the dishes *themselves* don't need washing. Think about it. You may want to straighten or not straighten the rumple in the carpet, but the carpet *itself* is already done. The cancer *itself* doesn't need curing. The whole world is already done, whole, and perfect—including you. How does God want the universe to be? Exactly the way it is in *this* moment.

Enlightenment is the end—the end of human suffering, the end of *your* suffering. Once you taste this perfection, your life will change. There's so much love, peace, and celebration that your heart can't contain it all, and you will have to share it. Can this experience of the end last forever? Yes, it is possible! But in fact, it almost never does for anyone. At some point, you get to return—not to the middle, but to the beginning and the discovery of what it means to live a genuinely spiritual life.

Chapter 3

Awakenings

A spiritual awakening can happen at any age, whether you are prepared for it or not. In fact, preparation is a hallmark of life in the middle. Let me ask you: what is it you're endlessly preparing for? What is it we all seem to be endlessly preparing for? When *will* you be good enough? When *will* you be done?

And then, in the midst of all of this preparation, you wake up—BANG—and you get to directly perceive the perfection of everything all at once, including yourself. If you were to read the fine print on the label attached to your awakening, it would say, "No preparation required." So the universe is not without a sense of humor—or irony.

Does this confuse you? How is it that no preparation is required *and* we're all demonstrating endless preparation? With this BANG, you get to notice that all of your preparation was not the cause of your awakening, but is simply that which preceded it. "Ah, yes," everyone says, "there was that." And then the phone rings, or the baby cries, and life in the middle resumes. The somethings in our lives once again demand our attention, and the wholeness of everything all at once slips away.

At any given moment, you *can* wake up in the present forever—regardless of any preparation. But from life in the middle, don't dismiss or disparage all the preparation you are doing. All that you have done and will do, for you, is what in fact precedes your awakening. Can it be any clearer than that? The actual life you are living is Source's path for *you*.

And because we all lose our connection with Source, spiritual awakenings—BANG—usually happen more than once. As my Tibetan teacher told me, when those moments of awakening bear fruit, collect them like pearls on a string and let them rest close to your heart.

Grinding pencils

The first pearl on my string came when I was eleven years old. Was I prepared? Well…sure. My young life was full of stress, and my often-stated goal to myself was to somehow ease my mother's suffering. I did everything I could, but nothing seemed to work. I was more than ripe for what came one winter morning in seventh grade.

Standing in the far corner of the classroom, I sharpened my pencil. This was my third trip to the pencil sharpener in the last thirty minutes, and I was not alone. There had been a steady stream of seventh graders trooping to the sharpener for the last half hour. Who could have predicted such an epidemic of worn-down and broken No. 2 pencils?

Mr. Boar sat at the front of the room in his blond oak chair, behind his blond oak desk, trying not to notice. This was our study time, but no one was studying. After dreary months of gray and rain, we were mesmerized by the first snow of 1962 in the Willamette Valley of Oregon. Winter was swirling right outside the large casement windows of our room. The wind was rising—and so was Mr. Boar, again.

Thirty minutes earlier he pulled down the long canvas window shades, hoping to contain us. Do you remember window shades? They had the hilarious or irritating feature (depending on how old you were) of suddenly jumping straight up in the air and recoiling themselves with a lot of flapping and banging. Usually this happened right after Mr. Boar adjusted them. Or it could happen any time, without warning, and with such force that the shade would dislodge from the friction mounts, hurl itself from the top of the window frame, and land on my classmates in an apparent murder-suicide attack. At these times we would gasp and laugh, enjoying our break from classwork. The survivors climbed back into their desks, the boys with a look of expected admiration, having met and defeated their old foe. Mr. Boar usually chuckled and swore under his breath (we delighted in that) and gathered up the wayward shade.

Lowering the shades that morning was successful—briefly. It stopped us student captives from randomly popping up from our desks to steal a look outside. The only place left to see out was the back corner of the room where the pencil sharpener was mounted on the windowsill, preventing the shade from being lowered all the way. It was possible for students to squat slightly at the knees while sharpening pencils and see snow accumulating on the massive branches and arthritic roots of the giant chestnut trees.

In moments of spiritual enlightenment, everything all at once is experienced as perfect, including you.

Mr. Boar stood up, hands on hips, head bent forward with an air both determined and resigned. The class paused; we could not predict his next move. He looked directly at me, as I ground my soft-leaded pencil to a nub. "Everyone back to your desks," he said. "Steve, sit down and write five hundred words on what you saw outside. Don't leave your desk until you are done."

Five hundred words!? I hadn't written five hundred words in my whole school career. No one looked my way with sympathy or any other emotion. They all got the message—and no one wanted to join me as a sacrificial lamb.

Looking down, I saw my eleven-year-old fingers gripping the stubby yellow pencil above a blank sheet of paper. "Blank mind," I wrote, and suddenly the window shade in my mind jumped open; I was hurled inward on a flood of images, landing safely in the branches of the chestnut trees and what I saw was ... snow. "Gray snow covering up," I wrote, "covering up everything that man has destroyed and changed ..."

As I calmly wrote, memories and images flooded in. I wrote down the images—man destroying the natural world—but the memories were all personal: my three sisters and I standing in line waiting to be beaten, our pants pulled down around our ankles. My mother's boyfriend used the broad black leather belt until we begged and screamed for him to stop. I remembered the terror I felt waiting in line for my turn, amplified by my sisters screaming and begging and crying. Our bodies were young and small and impotent. We fidgeted and danced around, small hands flapping at our mouths and teary eyes. There was nothing we could do. There was nothing I could do. We were sharing the same fate as the trees and air and water.

Over the course of an hour, I wrote nine hundred words in what was probably the most natural and uncharacteristic event of my young life. I was not a good student, but shy and continuously distracted by the abuse at home. On that day, I wrote from a place that was me *but much bigger than me.*

The words were written and the hour passed. I walked to Mr. Boar's desk, and he took the pages, his surprise showing. As he read, he kept looking up at me, seated at my desk across the room.

And I *saw* him. It seemed I could watch each individual whisker on his face growing. I knew and understood him, and all those around me, without words, and it must have shown. "If I hadn't watched you with my own eyes," he told me when he returned the pages, "I wouldn't have believed it was possible you wrote this."

Later, I agreed with him. How could this have been me? But not that day. On that day, I saw a *truth*, and wrote it without tears or blame. In fact, for several days this place of noticing and acceptance *was me.*

My first awakening deeply affected those around me, and my life changed. Mr. Boar saw the potential in me and supported me the rest of the year. I had his attention and his love. Every day at school I got to experience what it was to have an adult who was fundamentally interested in my well-being. For some time, good teachers became my role models. I looked forward to going to school and doing well (and it turned out I was really bright). My awakening had opened a direct connection to an inner wisdom that exceeded my years. I realized I had a life separate from my mother's and became committed to my own life. I became more outspoken—even opinionated. My mother and her boyfriend noticed that I was no longer an easy target. I was never beaten again, and I no longer looked to them to know who I was.

When the shades are drawn and you have only a narrow view of reality, then open to that place where you can view the wholeness of any life situation, including yours. You'll know you are there when you calmly sense everything around you, both the order and the chaos. From this place, whatever needs changing will change, sometimes spontaneously but more likely over an extended period of time. In fact, multiple awakenings are usually required.

Who's burning the hash browns?

Whatever you've read about awakening, it is never smooth. In fact, a spiritual awakening may at first feel like the farthest thing from clarity, love, and wholeness. In the beginning it may more closely resemble depression and even psychosis. My awakening as an adult lasted over twelve years, including eight years in a classic "dark night of the soul." During this time, I had moments and hours, even days or weeks, where I crossed over into enlightenment. But in each case, my realization faded and I returned to life in the middle, consumed and obsessed with all the particulars.

In the spring of 1988, I was living on the Oregon coast when my years of successful accomplishment and accumulated stress blossomed into a full-fledged spiritual awakening. For the previous two years, my sleep had become increasingly interrupted; for the last five months I slept maybe fourteen hours *a week*. Yet I was determined to keep my children together, keep my two successful businesses flourishing, and survive my divorce after twenty years of marriage. At that time, I had no idea what was happening to me, and I just wanted it to go away. But the universe, it seemed, had other plans for me.

The fastest route to knowing God is to know the present. The fastest way to love God is to love the present.

I enjoyed cooking hash browns and eggs for my two daughters on Saturday mornings, if their schedules and moods let me. Meadow, at fifteen, was independent and a promising artist. Cedar, at twelve, wrote melancholy poetry and song lyrics that were disturbing and revealing at the same time. As much as I loved them, I was losing them and they knew it.

Standing over a sizzling pan at the kitchen stove, I felt how rough the previous night had been on me. I experienced deep physical pain in my calves for hours. Around 3 a.m., the pain finally shot up and through my body and exploded in my brain. It felt like ten thousand volts of electricity—a supernova in my head. Just as this was subsiding, I felt a presence in my bedroom doorway. I checked to see if I had become lucid in a night dream—I hadn't. Soon two beings surrounded by a mist floated in and approached the foot of my bed....

Shaking myself out of my reverie, I looked up as Meadow walked into the kitchen. "Dad," she said, "the hash browns are burning big time—and what's *wrong* with you?" Right behind her came Cedar, her round face matching her short, round body. "Yeah, Dad," she said. "What's the deal?"

How could I explain this to my family and friends?

At first, the only explanation I could understand for the insomnia, voices, and visions was stress. So I visited the local doctors and psychologists in the small coastal town of Oregon where I lived. The doctors prescribed sleeping pills, which worked for a while, but usually left uncomfortable side effects. The counselors suggested that I was under a lot of stress and should relax. I agreed, but how? The not sleeping and incredible experiences were disturbing. One counselor actually asked me *not* to return because my experiences upset *him*.

So I explained to my kids that I was under a lot of stress, that my increasingly worn demeanor and daytime crying spells would pass, and I would get back to being the same old dad they had always known. At first I believed it would pass—and it might have, except that every night I became a traveler in other universes. Part of the time I was living in the jet stream of the unconscious—dense, turbulent, and thick with meaning. Other times I was in realms of incredible spaciousness, full of light, being coached by ethereal beings. I never knew what was in store next.

Sometimes it took hours to pull myself together after a night of intense dreams and waking visions. In the morning, my kids saw me discombobulated. I desperately tried to be what I wasn't anymore—normal, focused on everyday activities, and at peace.

Some mornings as I drove Cedar to school, I tried to answer her questions. We talked about dreams, hers and mine. I discovered that waking visions sounded too much like hallucinations—that Dad really was going crazy—so I didn't mention them again to my kids until much later.

I asked others about their dreams. I met a few who remembered and recorded their dreams every night, but no one was having these kinds of experiences. The more I read, the less it seemed that I was experiencing simple stress and insomnia.

My curiosity increased, and over the following months I read everything I could find. After a long search, it became clear to me that I was experiencing a *typical* spiritual awakening. The stories other people told showed that my awakening fit a broad pattern. I learned that awakening can be a long process, producing experiences that profoundly interrupt your otherwise ordinary life. Having lucid dreams, hearing voices, and experiencing waking visions are not at all unusual during a spiritual awakening.

Of course, experiences like these *are* unusual and almost always threatening to you, your family, and friends. Their typical response is to advise therapists and therapy (which can be useful) or more likely medication. What is lacking is the guidance of a teacher. Does everyone have to have a teacher to negotiate their spiritual awakening and realize enlightenment? Probably not, but most people aren't going to be able to do it alone. Besides family and friends, your ego gets in the way—the doer, the thinker, the part that's ambitious is almost always entrenched in illusion. This is when life will probably supply an explosion to dislodge your illusions. Do I recommend explosions? No. But I recognize that so often life shakes you hard, and these explosions can be the beginning of a genuine awakening. Often at this point people ask, "Why me, God?"

•   •   •

Right in the middle of your accomplishment and stress, where is God? For some of you, the questions may be, "Is there even a God? If there is, is God responsible for my suffering?" The answers for now are "yes"; I won't even suggest that your suffering isn't real. Can the God of your religion ease your suffering? Yes, God can. But what if your suffering doesn't end and your life in the middle begins to include many of the elements of a spiritual awakening—voices, visions, unusual body sensations? Is God responsible for these experiences? Is God punishing you?

Someone once asked me if indeed God was punishing him with his spiritual awakening. The answer is "no." You have to understand that the God that provides spiritual awakening is not the God of your religion. Most people who practice religion will never achieve spiritual awakening because religion is not about knowing God *directly*.

Religion is about providing its followers with rules to safely guide them through their time on earth without anything too unsettling happening. Religion provides a kind of safety net or fence to separate you from "nonbelievers," which may well include your neighbors, your friends, or even other family members. From my perspective, religion is within the realm of separation and illusion.

That's why Source provides these big explosions—they dislodge the deep illusions. Sometimes it takes a shaking to get a person to the point of "I really don't know." From a place of not knowing, they *must* return to noticing what actually is, apart from their illusions.

Knowing God

In your life in the middle, you may well have a working relationship with God. God may guide your decisions and give you peace of mind. But when a genuine spiritual awakening shakes you, your past relationship with God, just like everything else in your life, will be inadequate for what you're experiencing. Prayer as you've known it will not be sufficient to appreciate the overwhelming disorientation and experience of loss. During midlife passage, pastors, priests, ministers, and monks can end up shaken and seeking help, just like everyone else.

If you are seeking a religious experience of God in the classical ways of prayer and meditation, there's nothing wrong with that, but take a closer look. Does the experience include everyone, or does it separate you from others?

If you have an experience of God within a religious practice, the risk is that it facilitates separation. When an experience of God is more religious than spiritual, an arbitrary separation is created between the experience of the divine and everything else. Then you have your God or your savior or your guru, and all the rest of it is, in some important degree, "wrong." This is the down side of religion. It leads to holy wars and persecution and religionism.

Along your spiritual development, it may be important to create a fundamental distinction between God and everything else. But with enlightenment, this distinction is seen to be arbitrary.

If you have a belief in God, consider that Source is not the God of your beliefs. To know God, you must give up all of your romantic ideas, fantasies, and beliefs about God. In the end, they will only come between you and the presence of Source. Am I completely disparaging of theories, romantic fantasies, ideas, and beliefs? No. There is a place in the spiritual life for these. They serve to bridge the gap between living in the present with presence and experiencing anything less. Ideas and beliefs can point you in the right direction. They can provide a ration, albeit meager, to sustain you on your journey. But don't confuse this with the main course. I understand why and how beliefs can become serious: because the gaps are so wide between moments of living in the present. But when presence is only temporarily lost and often regained, the gaps narrow and beliefs and ideas and fantasies become a playground, not a debate.

There are days on end when my physical body and my mind and spirit are filled with ecstasy. If I were a religious person, I would probably call it divine ecstasy. But I let it last just as long as it does, knowing that it's going to pass anyway.

You may have a vision of God or you may get to hear God's voice in your mind or in a dream. You may have a very profound feeling of a presence that you could only describe as a supreme being. But for almost no one do the visions or the sound of God's voice continue nor does that overwhelming, indescribable, feeling-presence persist. For almost everyone who has these experiences, they fade. What is it that doesn't fade? What is it that persists? What has your attention?

In my experience, the quickest route to God is not through an overwhelming, transcendental experience, although that may happen—and I suggest that you say "thank you" if it does *and* let it go.

Instead, the quickest route to God is through *these three dimensions*. From my perspective, Source has left all of these clues and cues everywhere for us, absolutely everywhere. Source has set it up so that we are always in three dimensions surrounded by stuff. As you sit feeling the weight of the book in your hands at home or in a coffee shop or listening to the tape on your drive to work, what has your attention? From my perspective, spirituality is not a question of worshiping God; it's more a recognition of attention.

The fastest route to knowing God is to know the present. The fastest way to love God is to love the present. In this moment, how does God want the world to be? In this moment, just the way it is. If you want to align your will with God's will, best to pay attention to how things actually are. So begin by returning your attention to these three dimensions.

Stirred, not shaken

Earlier, I said that I don't recommend explosions. But when you fail to notice and accept how things are, you invite an explosion. Is God punishing you? No. This is just the way the system works. It's like driving down the freeway and failing to notice your temperature gauge has gone up. Everything's fine, you say. Then the car starts bucking and weaving. The wind must be blowing hard today, you say. Aren't you inviting an explosion? Isn't Source doing everything it can to get your attention?

Throughout your day, Source regularly shifts your attention to notice these three dimensions. When you do not follow the shift, you demonstrate your preference for having your world be some other way than God has it. When you do not follow the shift, you bump your head or trip over the door sill, don't you? Is it any better to drive down the road and never take your attention off your temperature gauge? No. Wouldn't this also invite disaster?

It is possible to have the experience of awakening without profound stress. You can be stirred, rather than shaken. This is the role of the enlightened teacher—to shift your attention, just like Source does. Then everything becomes a learning experience and an opportunity to wake up. You don't need to wait until you see the light on your death bed to experience this. Don't misunderstand; great personal transformation *can* happen in the presence of literal death, profound loss, and suffering. *But this same transcendence can happen through a series of small deaths, small separations, and small losses.* You can be stirred, rather than shaken.

For a genuine teacher, enlightenment brings with it the experience of noticing—when you can't *not* notice what is going on in the world, in people, and in the realm of spirit. Noticing "what is," exactly as it is, has immense power to effect change. In the moment, it's that little step that the student doesn't recognize, rather than the big change that they're sure they must make, that will stir them rather than shake them. A genuine teacher can bring tremendous noticing to every aspect of your life and help you avoid the big explosions.

Imagine you've just served up your plate from the buffet line and everything on it is just the way you want it. You sit down at a table with other students, friends, and teachers. Before you take the first bite, everyone receives the

You can be stirred, rather than shaken.

instruction to pass their plates to the person on their right and enjoy their new meal. I've witnessed people with years of spiritual training get angry and upset over this exercise. Is it possible to experience this small loss, to let go of a small preference in the moment, and experience transcendence? Yes.

Letting go of dozens then hundreds then thousands of small preferences over time will allow you to begin to perceive not just what *you* need in *your* life, but what the life situation all around you requires—what the universe requires from you, apart from any of your preferences. Will this dramatically reduce the stress in your life? Yes. Of course, along the way you will get sick or change careers, or someone close to you will die. And you may well have the opportunity to face your death. But these need not be explosions. Through noticing and letting go, you will experience them with grace and presence.

Along with helping the student avoid the explosions, the teacher also helps the student discover the teacher inside. I notice that people intuitively know enough to not surrender to the small parts of their personality—those that are easily bored, greedy, peevish, whiny, or jealous. Nothing is wrong with these "small" parts. They are a necessary part of being Only Human. The teacher's job is to notice the parts that are Only Human and to also notice and encourage the inner teacher when it shows up. When that inner teacher finally takes permanent residence in the student's body, the teacher's job is half done.

Are you ready for enlightenment?

Of the few enlightened people I've met and spent time with, not one of them demonstrated all human foibles at once, *but they all embodied some.* Were they "pure"? Pure what? Forget pure. Were each of them enlightened? Absolutely. Were they still human? Well, are they still in a body? Of course. Might there be something left for them to do here on earth? Absolutely, but they weren't just

Only Human. There was a palpable difference between them and the rest of us.

This can be a kind of spiritual dilemma for students. People want their teachers to be both "pure" and Only Human. They want them to be on the one hand infallible and on the other hand not that much unlike them.

During the times I've spent both visiting and studying with enlightened people, and eventually living closely with a teacher, I discovered how the humanness and compassion of the teacher could at times blind me to their enlightenment. My last teacher seemed to be in one moment the best buddy I ever had as we worked together on simple tasks—preparing a meal or fixing the lawnmower. In the next moment, still awash in his attention, I began thinking to myself, "So this is enlightenment. Maybe he's not so special, after all."

And suddenly, there seemed to be a vast distance between us. In an instant, I felt left behind, cut off, and possibly tricked. What happened? I understand now that he was aware of everything that I was thinking and feeling. When familiarity showed up, and I tried to make us equal by lowering the bar, he instantly knew and demonstrated "no" without word or gesture. He just *looked* at me—appreciating all I was going through, still demonstrating his love for me *and* his commitment to not mislead me. My response in those moments was confusion, disorientation, anger, and resentment, in that order. I wanted to run and hide my limitations, but he didn't. He saw and included everything. That's what an enlightened being does—celebrates everything, includes everything. In that moment, I couldn't celebrate my limitations. At these times, I wished that he would just lower the bar. Later, upon reflection, I was so thankful that he hadn't.

I now recognize that to lower the bar is to mislead. The role of the teacher is to accept you as you are, work with exactly what you bring, and to not ask of you any more than what you can do in the moment. But when I was thinking, "So this is enlightenment," I stopped demonstrating my natural enlightenment, and he immediately got it. For him to continue as if I were would be to mislead me.

Today, I describe it this way: before enlightenment, familiarity breeds contempt; after enlightenment, familiarity breathes content. When familiarity shows up, you must be willing to let it go. You and your teacher are not equal. This is one of the ways that the student demonstrates he is ready for enlightenment.

· · ·

What else do you have to give up to be enlightened? To make the leap, you must give up your next thought—about anything, including enlightenment. Want to make yourself crazy? Think too much about the value of not thinking. Do you see the humor there?

If you see it, can you laugh? And if you laugh, can you let go of even that and go bowling? Or climb a tree in your saffron robes?

"Easy," you might say. "What else do I have to give up?"

Your next feeling. If it's hard enough to imagine what it is to not think, it's even harder to imagine what it is to not feel. In this context, the English language doesn't allow me to describe "not feel" and not mean "unfeeling" or numb. When I suggest that students not feel what they would normally feel in the next moment, what they think I mean is "be unfeeling." Would you describe someone who is enlightened as unfeeling? No! When I say you won't be troubled by what you feel, that's not the same as being numb. Thinking too much will make you crazy; can I suggest to you that feeling too much will make you crazy, too? Enlightenment is also closer than your next feeling.

If you can entertain that it is useful to notice the pause that precedes thinking, consider that it is just as useful to experience the pause that precedes feeling. Do you hear the double meaning in the word "feeling"? In our language, feeling both describes physical sensations and emotions. This is the Only Human experience of confusing the two, but along the way the fusion gets taken apart. With enlightenment, it has to. With enlightenment, you get to return to that place where thinking and feeling are not split. There, you can notice physical sensations and entertain the birth of an emotion. Check it out. Every strong emotion requires that you take the situation personally and you experience one or more sensations somewhere in your body, probably in one of your organs. It could be a tight gut, an aching heart, or a throbbing headache.

What precedes the next thing you would normally think and feel is enlightenment. That's the doorway to not being addicted to what you'd normally think or feel—your automatic responses, beliefs, and emotions.

Feeling, as well as thinking, fragments reality. Wholeness, reality, and enlightenment are not feelings or states of mind. If being Only Human is where reality and illusion overlap, then the direct non-personal experience of enlightenment is no longer the overlap. The overlap disappears and you get to be more than Only Human. Can states of mind accompany this? Sure. Can profound thoughts accompany this? Sure. Can subtle *and* overwhelming feeling states accompany this? Sure. But reality *itself* is not a state of mind. Enlightenment *itself* is not a state of mind—or feeling.

When I appear to discount feeling states, people who are in an emotional ringer pay close attention. What I'm describing sounds like relief from intense or difficult emotions. Others who are numb through depression or withdrawal may conclude they are on the right track—that awakening means avoiding feelings. They may even decide that it's good to keep feeling less and less. Other people whose hearts and minds are a little clearer may get upset because I seem to be discounting their feelings. Some worry that they may be left detached, lofty, and removed from the world and the human predicament. On your spiritual journey, you may experience yourself as uncaring or unfeeling, but that's not the fruit of the experience. That's not what I'm pointing to.

All of these responses are "off the mark" because the pause before feeling must be experienced to do its work on you. Afterward, this experience can only be described as *not a personal experience*. It is this non-personal experience that is at the heart of enlightenment. That's the part that makes us more than Only Human.

Now and then, there are some few people who upon hearing this neither think much about it nor experience any "feeling" disturbances. They may say, "My mind is empty and it feels great"—but in describing the spacious pause, why give it feeling adjectives? The profound experience of spaciousness is *not personal*. It's not "you" having the experience.

One reason why it's so hard to describe profound spiritual experiences is that all of your thinking and feeling states are conditioned to our common experience and description of reality. Yet we know that what we ordinarily experience as reality is at best a profoundly abbreviated shorthand for what really exists. Taking part in reality has less to do with personal experience and more to do with non-personal, direct participation in these three dimensions.

So to become enlightened, give up your next thought and feeling to reside in that pause—the non-personal experience of spaciousness before thinking and feeling arise.

•   •   •

What else is required? Give up doing.

This goes back to the yoga of accomplishment. Can you care for the poor and the sick without a personal agenda? Can your satisfaction be independent of the outcome? When we are stuck in the middle, this yoga of accomplishment is always about measuring, and somehow you may not measure up. Ambition is tricky business, particularly spiritual ambition. Spiritual ambition—isn't that a hoot? Do you see the humor in it? Yet I meet this everywhere I go. Spiritual ambition is relentless and pervasive—doing its job of teasing and testing and trying the individual, backing up the human being with its paradox and contradiction, until they have nowhere to hide and must leap backward, past their insecurity *and* their security. Where do they land? In the pause before thinking and feeling. The mind can't swallow whole this pause, and yet enlightened speech and action always follow from that place that precedes thinking and feeling. Where else could it come from?

This is part of what can be frustrating living and working with enlightened spiritual teachers. Their teachings keep changing. They may sound as if they're contradicting themselves. They may demonstrate the most delightful incompetence. Why won't they just stay put? If they would remain in one place long enough, they could be understood, couldn't they? They could be codified and you could discover their principles, their methods, and you could get it right. You could think the right thoughts, feel the right feelings, and finally rest assured.

This is the birth of religion. And it may be inevitable that any "successful" spiritual teacher will give birth to yet another religion. Religion has been described as a vehicle for those who are not going to wake up in this lifetime. No matter how hard they work, no matter how much they meditate, or pray, or expand their breath, or stretch their bodies, they will not discover the spacious mind and heart that precedes everything in wholeness, perceives everything all at once. Why is it that religion so often becomes spiritual politics, or even secular politics, with its rules and laws and punishments and favors and bribes and purchased advantage? It is these very rules and precepts that so many are seeking, and religion gives them what they want. It does not require of them an ongoing, genuine spiritual inquiry.

What if, as human beings, we could celebrate being Only Human *and* be more than Only Human? Are you interested in occasionally stepping outside of rules and laws and principles and right and wrong and good and bad? As you scramble and stumble and sprint up the mountainside of life, would you occasionally like to enjoy the view from the top? What if I told you that to reach the top you would need to give up your ideas of everything—all of it. Temporarily and instantaneously let go of everything you normally feel about anything.

I've been asked, "But would it be a pleasant or unpleasant feeling, this view from the top of the mountain?" Even after saying all that I've said, I do deeply understand how it is that a human being can still ask that question. Everyone would like to give up the unpleasant feelings, the difficult emotions, and the troublesome thoughts. But what about the opposite and complementary feelings and emotions and thoughts?

Imagine you're sitting in the dentist chair, and he's about to remove the eyetooth of thought and the molar of feeling. You may even be proud and exhausted that you made it this far, you found the dentist, you found your way into the chair, and you said yes I am ready. The dentist says fine, lean back. Wait, you say, is this going to hurt? Can you give me something for the pain? The dentist replies, what pain? I haven't done anything yet. You say, the pain I will feel when you pull the eyetooth of thought and the molar of feeling. You even suggest that you would do fine with the prick of the syringe so that you do not feel the greater pain. The dentist replies, I have no syringe. I have nothing to numb you with.

.   .   .

How do you negotiate with enlightenment? What can you pack for the trip? I advise packing very little. Sort through all of your belongings—past, present, and future. Select only those that are of value to you. How will you know what's of value to you? It should be fairly obvious. It is only that which gets you going in the morning and that wakes you up in the dead of night. Let's call these your actual motivations and actual worries. Leave behind all your ideas. Ideas are like theories, even true theories, but they only offer descriptions. They are never what is being described. You are what is being described. What you are demonstrating is the price of admission. Learn to notice what it is you actually demonstrate. Your closest friend and your best enemy share this in common: they see what it is you demonstrate apart from any thinking or theory you have about yourself and the world around you.

Have you ever visited with a genuine spiritual teacher and felt lighter and more loved and more seen, and felt the measure of possibility? And perhaps through the rarest of invitations, you go to live close to him or her. Remember what it was of value that you packed? This is all that the teacher is interested in. He may well share with you your delight in your ideas and theories and perceptions, carefully and lovingly skimming them off the top of your mind and heart as you begin the immediate process of stewing. From time to time, you can smell something cooking. Sometimes it smells so pleasant; other times it smells like raw compost. What's cooking, you ask the teacher. You, is his reply. Which do you prefer, the rich savory smell or the smell of the compost? Let go of the preference and you are already halfway there. The teacher gently stirs to avoid any sticking and expertly turns the heat up and down to reveal what it is that you demonstrate, what it is that all your previous lifetimes have brought to this lifetime, this week, this day, this moment. What are you demonstrating? All else will be revealed as mere froth. This is what you have to offer the teacher; this is what gets revealed and transformed. But almost no one wants to see or have others see what it is they demonstrate, what it is that their best enemy and their worst friend have seen all along, though perhaps not seeing all of it.

During my dark night of the soul, I remember going to a wonderful mentor, an older man and teacher whom I respected but could not connect with. And I asked him, "Do you like me?" He said, "I'll get back to you on that." After several days, he called my home and agreed to talk to me about this. He explained that this was one of the bravest questions anyone had ever asked him. He asked me if I was ready to hear his answers. I said yes, because it was more important for me to know what he saw in me and felt about me than it was for me to defend and maintain my view of myself. For the next twenty minutes, he sobered me. He undid the intoxication of self-importance and self-defense and self-justification.

He cut through all of my stories of why I was how I was. He did so with the most amazing dispassion. He returned the same courage in dealing with me that I had shown in asking my question. He did not attack, and he did not spare or soften the truth. Afterward, we walked and talked and ate lunch at a café. We did not review what he had said. I had traded what I valued most—my self-image—and I got the bargain.

Chapter 4
Avocado Dialogues

I have discovered I have little to say unless someone asks a question; then, out of the stillness of everything all at once, the universe hands over a slice of the avocado—a piece of the unimaginable everything that an ordinary human being can digest. Do not be fooled, however; despite the apparent something being offered, that big green avocado is still whole, falling from the tree. The invitation is always there to catch it.

Much of this book comes directly from these sorts of avocado dialogues and conversations with friends, students, and visitors during public talks, workshops, and retreats. In compiling the book, I chose to preserve some of these conversations virtually as they occurred—so much more is revealed in this way.

In the following dialogues, comments from the audience are preceded by "Q." Subheadings are used for clarity within a conversation, and symbols are used to signal the start of a different dialogue. More conversations follow in later chapters of the book.

Something and everything

Q. If illusion isn't real, why can't we all just wake up and be done with it? What's stopping us?

We all can, as you say, "wake up and be done with it." Do you really want to know what is stopping us? Do you really want to know what is stopping *you*? You may not like the answer.

Q. Sure, I want to know.

Nothing is stopping you. Absolutely nothing. Any other questions?

Q. But something must be stopping me. I've been pursuing enlightenment for too many years to be put off with an answer like that.

Responses vary with that answer. Some people become angry, others sad or frustrated, some even laugh. A very few simply stop thinking, sometimes for a few moments or *much* longer. Whatever the response is, that response *is* the next "something" that happens between you and your perception of enlightenment.

Q. Are you saying that my anger is stopping me? I was doing fine until you upset me.

I did, didn't I? I upset you. I will accept that. In this moment, I am what is stopping you from awakening. Does that help?

Q. No, not really. Wait, even as I say that, I know that's not what I mean, or rather that's not what I want to say. Look, sometimes everything is so clear to me and I'm sure that I'm done with searching and then some little thing happens and it's gone. I get so frustrated. I've gone to lots of workshops, done emotional work, and nothing helps for long.

What you are saying is a perfect description of what it is to be Only Human, caught between illusion and reality, and on the spiritual path. If it brings you any comfort, you are not alone. Whether what interrupts our clear seeing is frustration, or anger, or jealousy, or the doorbell, or romance, or a brilliant idea, or the baby, or cancer, or the whistle of the tea kettle, all of these are the *somethings* that fill our lives. But in your moments of spiritual enlightenment, *everything* all at once is experienced as perfect. True?

Q. Yes. I would say it a little differently, but that's it.

Human beings are exactly in the middle, caught between these moments of spiritual enlightenment and the ordinary world of separation, suffering, and illusion. Since only human beings would ask, "What is the point of illusion," they would have to be in the middle, wouldn't they?

So from that place right there—from your place right there in the middle of it—*what is stopping you?*

(He searches for an answer, but has no reply.)

Is reality stopping you? Is "everything" stopping you? Check it out.

Q. No.

Are the somethings stopping you? Is nothing stopping you?

Q. Illusion is stopping me.

Illusion is stopping you. Has illusion done its job well?

Q. Yes.

And yet you are awakening. By your own account, you have had the experience of spiritual enlightenment—the direct perception of reality. And having had it once, you have devoted the rest of your life to finding it again. True?

Q. Yes.

So it would seem that reality is doing its job, as well. I know what you're thinking, that you still want to get rid of illusion, that illusion is the problem.

Is illusion the problem? Of course it is. And don't you want to get to the source of the problem? Don't you want to get to the source of *your* problems, *your* suffering? Of course you do; we all do. But how will you know when you're done? You will know that you've gotten to the source of the problem when all that is left is Source. Your illusions and the process of disillusionment is the only *path* that Source has given us. This path is awakening.

Before the spiritual path, illusions seem to just serve themselves, and your life might be mostly about accomplishment. This even includes personal growth. But once you're on a spiritual path, it becomes clear how vast and pervasive illusion is. But illusion could not do its job as well as it does without reality greasing the skids. This is the collusion between reality and illusion,

You will know when you've gotten to the source of the problem when all that is left is Source.

between Source and its expression.

Remember the somethings that show up to interrupt your spiritual experience of everything? That is Source expressing itself. Reality is what makes illusion possible because reality can *only* express itself in all the somethings. Every expression of what is real can only be in the realm of illusion or form. Illusion may be nothing, as you said, but it is always some expression of what is real.

Human beings are where illusion and reality overlap. The only way we will ever come to reality or enlightenment is through our illusions, because illusion is also what prevents us from deceiving ourselves. Illusions keep reminding us that we're not done. Once you're on a genuine spiritual path, you can't deny any more when you've been hooked and have fallen into the machinery of illusion—vanity, fear, selfishness, pettiness, greed. You cannot deny it. Illusion may show up as the next preference, the next frustration, the next denial of "what is." The next time you want to skip over accepting and loving "what is" and go directly to control, that's illusion reminding you that you're still on the path.

Sometimes human beings have a direct experience of reality and later tell themselves they're done. Maybe they are, and maybe they're not. If they are, illusion—all the somethings in their life—won't disturb the enlightenment. If they're not, illusion goes to work. Without that next illusion, that next something, you might come to believe you're done, that the awakening is complete, that you've ascended the mountain. So illusion keeps testing the product, and the testing is relentless. If there is a loose bolt or nut, illusion goes after it. Without the work of illusion, people on a spiritual path could fool themselves into thinking that their work was done when they are only halfway up the mountain.

"But I was in touch with reality," seekers say. They awaken for a moment or longer, maybe for a whole day, and then it's gone. But they're left with the afterglow, the echo, and so they try to hang on to it. Soon enough they leave the experience of enlightenment altogether and settle back into ordinary experience. So I ask you, what in that moment is "real"?

In that moment, when the experience of awakening is gone and they settle back into ordinariness, where is their attention? Where should their attention be? If your experience of enlightenment is a memory and you try to keep your attention on it, the most straightforward thing I can say is you're living in illusion. Why? Because your attention is on a memory and not in the present. Your attention is on "what isn't," rather than "what is."

The most straightforward way to return to the path of awakening is to acknowledge that illusion has your attention, then return your attention to where you are because you're always somewhere. Leave the world of two dimensions and thinking and return to noticing these three dimensions. Remember, the somethings around us in these three dimensions are our path to Source, our reminder of what is real.

Q. But I have heard other teachers say that the so-called objective world is an illusion and not real. Is that true?

Well, sure. These three dimensions are about something, and if you're a human being in a body, you live in the realm of somethings, of form. But don't ignore God's path for us.

Notice what you're demonstrating. If you're demonstrating anger, envy, or suffering, don't deny it. If you discover that you're off the path—if you discover that you can't directly return to everything— the way to get back is to return to noticing something, to get past your knowing and return to the direct perception of noticing.

Illusion also requires the experience of something specific. Isn't that a funny thing to say? The greater the illusion, the more one becomes convinced that something specific—either some physical object, or person, or emotion, or belief, or *anything*—is truly separate from everything else. How does something become so separate? Only in our thinking. In and of itself, nothing is that separate or that important.

When Gandhi was told how important he was—how indispensable he was—he blanched. When Ramana's followers said the same to him, he chastised them for being so foolish. Do you get it? Even the sages and saints with their remarkable wisdom did not see themselves

> *Only beings with bodies can perceive their own enlightenment.*

as anything special, unique, or important in and of themselves.

When we become obsessed or fixated upon anything—an idea, a song, a feeling, our body, or our individual lives—the natural wholeness of reality is lost to us. When we become fixated on just one behavior of someone and we become angry, infatuated, or despairing, we no longer perceive the rest of the person. They become for us only what we think and feel about them. The same is true when we become fixated on some idea or identity of ourselves.

When viewed from a place of separation, noticing something directly in these three dimensions restores some wholeness. From the place of perfection, wholeness is not an *attribute* of anything. Wholeness and perfection are the same thing, and this "thing" cannot be conceived by the mind, as you know. If your mind and emotions are not particularly spacious or open or loving, you can gain entry into wholeness through the somethings in your life. You can notice something specific in the room, like the glass of water, then notice the book, then notice the room, then notice yourself in the room. As you keep noticing, the context that all the somethings rest in will present itself, then you regain spaciousness—a clearer mind and a more open heart.

Q. Should we avoid the specific things in our lives?

No, this *is* how reality expresses itself. The somethings *are* the path back to Source. So from your perspective, have the best illusion you can possibly have. Become a magician of your illusions. Just remember that even though these somethings have as their source reality, they are still illusion. Play in illusion only as long as you do—but always return to Source.

Q. But wait, isn't God in everything around us?

Yes, God is in everything. That's my point. But that is not what anyone means when they say it. What people mean is that a piece of God is in all the somethings around them. But like Humpty Dumpty, you cannot take all these individual pieces and ever put them together again and return to everything. The pieces are in the realm of illusion—and this is good news. Illusion completely understands and fulfills the role of all these individual somethings operating together, yet separate. And it's true, isn't it? Almost everyone begins from a place of separation—from a place of separateness—and tries to control or influence what appears to be not whole or not loved or not accepted to satisfy their preferences for having things their way. With this, they do the work of illusion building. Why? Because illusions can be managed.

Source can never be managed, controlled, or facilitated … ever. Reality by itself is everything all at once, undivided, seamless—which ordinary human beings simply cannot grasp. The mind cannot do it. The human mind can only grasp something. Illusion is all the somethings in our lives. And it's all the somethings that we get hung up on, that we have preferences about, and yet make the lives we have possible.

Remember—without reality, illusion really is nothing. Without reality, there would be no illusion. There would be no striving or loss or accomplishments or stress or awakening. What is reality without illusion? Now consider this carefully. *Without illusion, reality also is nothing.* Isn't that an amazing thing to say? After you get it that reality without illusion is nothing, don't you have to celebrate illusions, every last one of them?

Q. I think I understand. Illusion is how reality does its job of awakening us. But where does this leave me?

Remember, it leaves you right in the middle. Your job is to let illusion *serve* your awakening, and to recognize that Source is here to *service* illusion. How can you put this into practice? In the same way: let your most important task be to learn how to be of *service* to others and, just as importantly, let others *serve* you. This is a vast learning and a vast practice; it can only be done with a clear mind and opening heart.

Why is service a task? Because it can feel so hard to be of real service to real people—people whom you take personally. This includes both the stinkers and those few truly wonderful beings who can also make your life "difficult" in their own special way, like spiritual teachers.

Become a magician of your illusions.

Once you get it that you are here to learn, the teachings *can* be hard. Sometimes it's as if the learning just never stops. Friends disappoint, lovers cheat, careers end or never get started, romance intrudes. And through it all, you can be of service to those around you simply by noticing people apart from what you may think or feel about them—all your judgments and desires and aversions. As often as you are able, just notice the actual human being in these three dimensions.

How do other people serve you? People serve to awaken you in all the thousands of ways that human beings show up for each other. Let them do their work. They are here to help you build your illusions—thought by thought, feeling by feeling—and then help you take them apart. How? By disillusioning you. Does disillusionment always have to hurt? Of course not. Does it in fact usually hurt? Yes. So remember compassion. Remember that you are doing exactly the same for others in their lives. You are at times loving and fulfilling and disappointing and interrupting and entertaining and teaching and grasping and clinging and abandoning and delighting. Aren't you? Isn't everyone else, too? And through it all, life just keeps massaging you. Sometimes it's relaxing; other times it bears down on those tight spots until the very tissue of your being must release, and you get to let go.

Shall I go on and on? Shall you go on and on? Doesn't almost everyone, almost all the time, just go on and on—careening or racing or plodding or dancing or stumbling or skipping or marching through life and its emotions? Of course we do. Does this list remind you of the somethings we talked about earlier? It should.

This is the flesh and bone of being Only Human. Is being Only Human at times playful and full of light? Yes. Is dancing and delighting and lightness closer to reality than the stumbling and frustration and darkness? Yes. Will both be finally transcended? Yes! Can they be transcended now, in this moment? Yes, they can—by accepting what is here and now, outside of right and wrong, good or bad. This is the heart and mind of noticing.

All my teachers succeeded in "relieving" me of illusions. It seemed that I was never who I "thought" I was, no matter what I thought! By their very existence, their very noticing and loving me for who I was, exactly as I was, I could not help but see through all these thoughts and beliefs about *myself* and *my* place in the world, and who had wronged *me*, and who had benefited from *me*. In living a genuinely spiritual life, all of what you think and feel will only take you so far. Noticing will take you the rest of the way.

When thoughts stick around long enough, they coalesce into preferences, expectations, and finally beliefs. Our beliefs (and feelings) usually find expression in the physical world as well as our mental worlds. So human beings have their worldly creations and their daydreams. This is the playground of illusion, a playground built out of all your interactions.

Illusion attempts to contain or slow down reality, just like a container where the interaction between molecules generates heat from friction. Likewise, all that you interact with—including other people, emotions, thoughts, ideas, and feelings—creates friction. This friction is illusion doing its job.

Hands down, people are your best source of friction. They can both keep you warm at night and make you a little crazy in the morning, and vice versa. So you say, "Argh!! I want a break!" And you take one. Soon enough, boredom sets in. There is not enough happening. So you watch TV, go on vacation, date, think about something interesting, and so on. More interactions lead to more learning, more teachings, more friction, more illusion. Isn't it great? Illusion is always there, ready to serve. What does it serve? It serves your awakening.

So stop denying the illusion when you live in illusion. That will make you less crazy. Stop denying reality. Stop ignoring "what is," exactly as it is. Start noticing and loving and appreciating "what is," outside of your or anyone's preferences. You will display your competence, and as your will becomes aligned with God's, you will live in perfection that does not deny the imperfection.

I've said that awakening requires a clear mind and open heart. Why an open heart? Because reality is always whole. Reality can only offer itself whole to human beings, like that ripe avocado that is falling from God's Tree of Life and caught in mid-flight, by you. Can you swallow it whole? Do you believe that is even possible? Be honest. Aren't you sure you would choke and die? This is the mind's response. Only an open heart can help a clear mind make the leap that enlightenment requires.

•   •   •

Q. When we "project" our qualities on to someone else, is that also illusion?

Yes, that is a kind of illusion. What is fascinating about projection is that while the individual may or may not have the quality we credit them with or blame them for, we almost always do have that quality.

But it is possible to notice and discover if that person actually has that quality. When you notice in this way, you also notice the rest of the person—the whole of the person. Then there is no blame or credit, as you would normally use those words. There is just that which is noticed, including the whole of the person or situation and yourself. You can notice yourself in exactly the same way.

This expansion of what is noticed to include more and more of the wholeness—to *feel* more and more whole—is quite natural. This is where we are all headed. This is following the stream of noticing that leads to the great river of reality and empties finally into the ocean—the Source and expression of great compassion.

What is real

Q. What's the point of illusions?

First, what does the question have to do with you?

Q. There are so many things that are not real. I'm not my body, I'm not my emotions, I'm not my preferences. If what I am is just being, then what is the point? Is there a point?

So let me ask you again: why do you care what the answer might be? You might want to check in with your body before answering.

Q. Because I want to know that there is something real.

Living a genuinely spiritual life does not ask you to deny the illusions that present themselves to you, or any of us. Nor does living a genuinely spiritual life ask you to deny the peculiar realness of each illusion. But when you are in a place of emotion—which, although you haven't said it, is what is propelling your question—illusions can be powerful.

When the illusion is going well, that may be a better time to ask, "What's the point?" If I asked you this question when all was going well, what would you say?

Q. I have no frigging idea.

And you might add, in that moment of well-being, that the question is irrelevant. I observe that people mostly ask "what is the point" or "what is real" or "what is the use of illusion" when their current illusion hurts.

When you were listing what is not real, you said you were not your body, not your emotions, not your preferences. Have you ever heard me say at any length that you are not your body?

Q. But the body does not endure, and you have said that only what is real endures.

Again you are demonstrating theory. Your body is an external event and is a magnitude more reliable than your thinking right now.

In fact, enlightenment is only for bodies. Only beings with bodies can perceive their own enlightenment.

I could say that illusion is the curriculum and you are in school, so become a student, but you already are. I have suggested that you become a magician of your illusions, and slowly you are. But none of this, in this moment, speaks to what is propelling your inquiry. Could it be that when you ask "what is the point of illusion," what you really want to know is that one of your illusions is real?

Q. Yes, it could be.

Have you forgotten what delight is?

Q. What? What did you say? I couldn't hear the question.

I agree. Have you forgotten delight and joy and genuine curiosity?

(She begins to softly cry and breathes more deeply.)

Q. I have no idea why I am so upset.

You may pursue the "why" questions for however long that you want, but from my perspective, the "why" questions suck. And they always have. For the next few moments, ask your brain to sort for delight, OK? I can no longer join you in that place where there is no delight, no joy, no genuine curiosity about "what is." You have an ability I don't have. So that's good news, isn't it?

(She laughs, and her body and emotions shift again.)

When you say, "Emotions aren't real," we both know what you mean. Emotions don't endure. They have a beginning, a middle, and an end. Just like moods, they are ephemeral. You might feel the rage of jealousy, and then it passes. And you get it—the emotions aren't real, and thank God you didn't believe that one, or at least didn't act on that powerful feeling, because now your heart is open and loving once again.

Then you think, "What about love—isn't love an emotion, too?" Could this be the illusion you want to know is real?

Q. Yes.

The feelings of love, compassion, peace, and joy do not survive enlightenment *as you know them*. But these emotions are much closer to enlightenment—to what is ultimately real—than feelings of anger, rage, envy, resentment, or fear. Love and compassion point the way.

Free will

Q. Do we have free will?

Some people don't like my answer to this question. But from my perspective, free will for human beings most resembles a multiple-choice questionnaire, where you didn't choose the questions and you didn't choose the possible answers. But among the two or three or four possibilities offered to you, you have your choice.

And that is the essence of free will, isn't it? Your ability to choose. Yet there is so much that you didn't choose. You didn't choose your DNA and all it determines for you. You didn't choose any of your cultural or environmental circumstances. You were born into the middle of a specific family and a specific culture at a particular time in history—all of which provides opportunities and limitations that were beyond your choice. In a very real way, all of this determines life's agenda for you as well as your curriculum while you're on the planet.

It has been suggested to me that as souls we "choose" our life circumstances before each incarnation, so we must accept in a useful way our responsibility for all that we "create." From the perspective of the soul this is true, but this does not increase our measure of free will. If before you incarnated you chose to return as a man with blue eyes and a lisp who is attracted to older women—well, okay. But did you also choose to spill coffee on the blue corduroy pants that you were wearing when you crossed your legs at two o'clock in the afternoon last Tuesday? If this and all the rest was chosen *before* you incarnated, you would not be much more than a preprogrammed being simply playing out your script. That doesn't sound like free will.

And what about your thoughts? Since thinking is the realm where choice takes place, it would be critical that you be able to choose what you think, wouldn't it? Yet as a practical matter, in the last hour did you choose any of the thoughts that showed up? I mean, did you reflect: "I will come up with three things to think about and choose one of those to consider." No. Thoughts just show up.

I have thoroughly checked this one out, and continue to inquire of my students and others whom I meet. I request that you also check this out on your own, after you are sure you understand what it is I'm saying. Let me know the results of your inquiry.

Here is an example. If I say to you "purple sailboat," notice the purple sailboat that showed up in your thinking. Got one? Good. Is your sailboat at dock or out on the water? Is it a wooden boat or a fiberglass boat? Are the sails up or down? Just notice you didn't choose any of the specifics; you never do. Your thoughts about a purple sailboat just showed up. In fact, you didn't "choose" to think about a purple sailboat; I chose it for you.

In much the same way, from the moment of birth you have been responding to stimuli from the world and everyone in it—from how your parents reacted to you, to what you studied in school and watched on TV. You didn't choose any of it. From my perspective, this is one of the most difficult parts for human beings living in this very realistic illusion: you are *endlessly responding* to both the external environment (including your own body) *and your thoughts*.

"Well sure," you might say, "Some thoughts just show up; perhaps lots of thoughts just show up, but I am sure that I can also choose thoughts." And I agree with you. After all, our ability to choose one thought or *behavior* rather than another is the basis for our moral, legal, and religious beliefs—plus it's one way we get to win arguments with our spouses! But try this experiment; think of an actress and write her name down. Do it now before we go on.

As you look at her name, let me ask you: what were your other choices when you chose her? As you think about this now, other possibilities may show up that didn't show up when you made your first "choice." If they do, notice if you chose them from yet other possible choices.

I've done this experiment with many people, usually by asking them to choose a place they would like to vacation. While they may well think of five possible places to go on vacation and choose one, the five options themselves just showed up. They did not choose them from ten other possibilities. All of that so-called "choosing" always takes place behind the scenes, outside of your awareness—which is just another way of saying that thoughts just show up.

But once you have two or more places to go on vacation, then you can choose one or more of them. This is our allotment of free will. This is your multiple choice questionnaire, where you did not "choose" the questions or the two or three or four possible answers, but once confronted with the possibilities you may well be responsible for your choice.

This may not seem like a lot of free will, and considering how much free will people think they have, the truth may disappoint. *But this is enough free will to get the job done.* This is all the free will that a human being needs.

Q. My unconscious mind may make choices for me, but they are still my choices.

Are they? From where I stand the "unconscious" isn't yours. How could it be? Your unconscious is the connection between the mind and body. You may be able to raise your arm or throw a baseball or dance the ballet, but can you tell me how you do it?

You might think, "I want to jump up in the air" and do so. But there were tens of thousands of electro-chemical and mechanical and as yet undiscovered processes at work, and you didn't control any of them. They were all outside of your awareness. This is the Mystery. Get it? This *is* Source at work. As you progress spiritually, you will take less and less credit for all that "you" accomplish, whether it is running, jumping, thinking, or feeling.

There is so little that is "new" in this world that most people would know if they were taking credit for someone else's ideas. Yet every time that something really new shows up, the inventor or writer or musician or philosopher or scientist says the most amazing thing. They say, "It wasn't me." It was inspiration, or the muse, or divine guidance. Edison would stare for hours at a blank chalkboard when discovering "his" inventions. Einstein wrote at some length about what happened to him as the ideas came forth.

Are you sure you want to annex the unconscious mind? What's next, *your* higher self, perhaps *your* angels, or *your* deities? How about *your* own personal God? Are you prepared to annex Source itself as your own?

These questions may sound silly, but they aren't—they get to the heart of spiritual inquiry, the heart of spiritual maturity. If you could let go of the unconscious as yours, the rest of your transformation might be easy.

Q. If our choices are so limited, why do we have free will at all?

You have free will so that at some time in this or some other lifetime, your awakening and eventual enlightenment become a real possibility for you. It becomes a choice on your multiple-choice questionnaire.

This is the value of teachers and sacred texts that invite you to step beyond your "individual" free will. They keep bringing up again and again this business of liberation, of surrendering your will to God's. Right in the midst of the realness of this consensual illusion, they intrude to stir us and rattle us and eventually wake us up.

After that, you have no free will. It is no longer a question of your individual franchise competing with the universe's or God's franchise. Every moment becomes a prayer, and simply noticing "what is," as it is, collapses into perfection. Any individual steps of accepting and appreciating what is are all expressed in the perfection, just as you are an expression of the perfection.

But this self-expression of perfection is not a personal experience. This is not your individual perfection or enlightenment apart from everything else that is. These are what I call non-personal experiences—where your individual will is irrelevant.

Surrendering to God's will

Q. You said a minute ago that every moment of life can become a prayer. What does that mean?

This gets to the nature of prayer and why it works and why it doesn't. When prayer works, your personal will has become aligned with God's will, and now both of you are voting for the same outcome. You are both voting for what's going to happen next. When your prayers are not answered, you have failed to perceive what's going to happen and voted for "what isn't." Since this gets to the heart of the human situation, you are not alone. So don't give yourself a hard time for failing to perceive the future. Remember, the future can only be imagined. It is of the same cloth as "what isn't"—a kind of daydream or fantasy.

If you want to increase the chances of your prayers being answered, keep your attention on the present. This is where all possible outcomes reside. The present contains *all the stuff* of which the future will be made—literally. When you notice and accept "what is," outside of right and wrong, outside of either approving or condemning "what is," you support reality. This is where the *power* of prayer resides—in reality. Prayer is the furthest thing from a daydream or fantasy. A prayerful life begins rooted and elevated in reality—in noticing and accepting "what is," exactly as it is.

From this place of noticing, accepting, and appreciating "what is," notice if there is anything different to pray for. If not, then simply continue to notice and appreciate everything, including the persons and situations that may be breaking your heart. This is prayer in action. This is surrendering your individual preferences to God's will.

As you practice this, two things happen. First, you begin to live more and more in perfection. You'll know it because it is often accompanied by the most profound sense of well-being. This is the natural consequence of supporting what is real—reality supports you. Pay attention to those moments of well-being and expand them.

Second, you may well get ahead of the curve just enough to perceive what it is that is going to happen next. If you do, then support that. If what's going to happen next includes some doing on your part, then you will find yourself doing it. This is natural competence. This is living responsibly.

To consider whether you are responsible for your actions is futile unless the considering is done from the present. Otherwise, to ask whether human beings are responsible—am I responsible—can only be a theoretical question that has nothing to do with reality and will only generate a theoretical answer. Living responsibly is supporting what is going to happen next. The present will never adequately respond to rules and beliefs that attempt to predict the future.

Q. Is the future fixed? Can it be changed?

The future can be changed, but it is the imagined future, not the actual future. Why would anyone want to change the actual future? To change the imagined future, use the normal ways, such as planning and taking concrete steps toward creating a life worth living. All of this is learning and mastering the rules of life. Since you live in this most incredible illusion, *become a magician—a magician of your illusions.* Magic is the successful manipulation of illusions from within illusion. This and more is your soul's work. But there is no "magic" in the present because there is no illusion.

As far as I can tell, people do not create their own reality, they create their own illusions. So I encourage everyone to have the best illusion possible. When you discover the rules of money, you become a magician of that illusion. You need money, so you create it. You need satisfying relationships, so you create them. People always blanch at that one because they want true love. There is such a thing as true love, but it can never be what you imagine. That is the problem. Everyone wants the kind of love that they imagine, but true love exists only in the present with actual human beings, not in the realm of imagination, fantasy, or daydreams.

Remember, you can only change the future that you imagine, but you can't change the actual future. The actual future *is* the present.

Q. Can I simply surrender my will to God's will?

Good question. Try it, right now. (Long pause.) What happened?

Q. At first nothing, or I should say I heard myself repeating the question in my mind over and over. Then I answered back that this is silly, and I would be embarrassed if something happened. Then I felt a swelling in my chest and stomach followed by fear, I guess. So nothing happened, right?

Each person has their own experience with this inquiry, but they are not exactly unique. What you describe is not uncommon. Every heartfelt request made of God or Source will generate a response. For now, let me say that the response you receive is almost always a mix of your personal psychology and *that which responds*. Do you have an intuitive sense of which was which for you?

Q. Well, hearing me talk to myself in my head is something I do pretty much. So that's just me.

Return to the swelling in your chest. Feel that again. (Pause.) What is that?

Q. I've felt this feeling before. It usually comes before a strong emotion, like love or sadness. Lately, it reminds me that I am pretty lonely.

Surrendering your will to the will of God is a surrender of the emotional heart, and your heart knows this. Our sense of separateness will resist surrendering for however long that it does. Its strongest resistance is fear, often preceded by anger, sadness, or despair, just to name a few. Do not push yourself. To do so is to commit a kind of violence on your self. In fact, don't *try* to surrender, simply notice. Simply noticing, as you are learning, will bypass that sense of separateness with its fearful resistance. And congratulations on noticing so much about your experience.

Q. I've heard you say that you don't even want the best for us—you want what's actually going to happen next.

Since I want what's going to happen anyway, I can drop the wanting and live with you in the present. Can you imagine a life free from wanting?

Part III
The Beginning

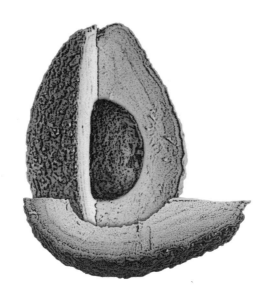

Introduction

The beginning is life after you have had a glimpse or longer of what it is to be Only Human and more, apart from what you may know or not know—even apart from what you may feel or not feel—about your life and all the life around you. This glimpse has been called enlightenment—swallowing that big green avocado whole.

Once you've done this, then what? Will this "non-personal" experience last? For almost everyone, the answer is probably not. You will almost certainly—from time to time, and probably much longer—forget the present. In fact, this is a good test to notice if you are living in the present. When you begin to describe enlightenment as *your own experience*, you'll know you have left the present. But the present won't have left you. It will have cut through all your previous experiences of yourself and the world around you, burned a pathway straight through your neural connections, and torched a route directly into your heart and head and belly.

What you will certainly forget will never forget you. Enlightenment will come tapping and whispering and pounding at the door of your everyday, Only Human self. Knowing that the door has been opened once or more, for a moment or longer, you will never be abandoned and you will never completely return to that illusory experience of separation that is life in the middle. You now have an opportunity to live without life being just about what you normally think and feel. You still have thoughts and feelings, but you won't believe them completely anymore. You'll know enough to trust the *pause* that precedes every thought and feeling. This is the beginning.

Chapter 5
Life in the Beginning

Once you have an experience of the end, you will still continue to experience spiritual awakening. For some period of time, however long it lasts, you may well have visions, hear voices, feel unusual body sensations and unpredictable emotions. This is progress. This is what gets to come next, yet it is also clearly an interruption from living in the present. As I said earlier, there is so much that serves to interrupt our clear seeing, from the over-drafted checking account to your next thought. To this list, you can now add most of what is considered "spiritual" experiences. No matter what you think of this, all of these spiritual experiences—however powerful and useful—will pass.

You will learn how to have these experiences and not get lost. Make no mistake—these are experiences. They have a beginning, a middle, and an end. You will learn that you can hear voices, see visions, and make room for them, and they will make room for you. Is all of this just your imagination? No. There really are other worlds that overlap our own. And so what? This business of awakening can go on right in the midst of making dinner for your family, taking care of friends, and watching your children play in the yard. When experienced from the present, any of this is no more disturbing or distracting than anything else. How is it that you stay present and entertain these experiences *and* let them entertain you? Because your attention now adds up to more than one hundred percent of what would seem to be possible.

Consensual reality requires that human beings divide their attention between the external—what they see and hear out there—and the internal—their pictures, sounds, and feelings inside of them. These pictures, sounds, and feelings make up our memories, associations, fantasies, and daydreams. Since our attention before enlightenment is divided between the external and the internal, the two always add up to one hundred percent. So daydreamers miss much of what is happening outside, and extroverts miss much of their interior life. But in each case, their attention always adds up to one hundred percent.

With enlightenment, your attention adds up to more than one hundred percent. I remember the first time my attention was seventy percent external *and* seventy percent internal—stunning clarity of mind and heart. How can this be? Because you have swallowed the avocado of enlightenment whole—you have been turned inside out, and what is external is now inside of you, and what is inside of you is now out there. When the boundary between internal and external dissolves, as it must for any spiritual experience to happen, your attention expands. If you don't expand when your attention does, you experience it as contraction, with everything that brings: fear, anxiety, and suffering.

As you learn to expand when your attention does, you'll discover there always has been a lot of space, a lot of open range, between thoughts and pictures and internal conversations. Silence and open space will begin to reign inside. Your attention on what is outside of you becomes rooted more in the space between objects, rather than the objects themselves. The silence out of which sounds arise becomes more interesting than the sounds themselves. You get it that the walls that surround you are just paper and dust and glue and don't separate you from anything, even if they are wood, concrete, or steel. They are just arbitrary but useful distinctions between inside and outside—internal and external.

Your sack of skin in which you appear to live is also an arbitrary but useful distinction. It does not separate you from what is outside of your skin. This means you can resonate with and borrow from, if you need to, the all-pervading silence in a rock concert and the spaciousness of a crowded football arena. It is almost all empty space and silence, you know. And those around you will begin to resonate with the open range and vast silence of your heart and mind.

If inside you it is crowded and noisy with conflicting thoughts and powerful emotions, then outside will appear as crowded and uninviting. No place for you out there, you say. No room. I must live alone, whether I want to or not.

Waking up in the present…forever

For those of you who have a dramatic experience of the end, when the experience disappears it will feel enormously painful to you at first. The contrast hurts. After your heart opens and mind clears, you have a fight with your wife, or a flat tire, or you just wake up one morning and it is gone. The cell door shuts. Life seems to be punishing you.

For some of you, you may be able to return to the experience of Avocado Consciousness once a year; for others it might be once a month or more. For those of you who start to experience the vastness more often, you say, "I forgot how wonderful life is. Now everything's coming up roses." But when there seems to be more thorns than roses in your life, you've forgotten the present. That's all.

Make no mistake: between times of grace, you may simply forget the present. That's just the setup for a while. That's just the way it is. As the amount of time increases that you spend in the vastness and silence, a bridge is being built that carries you through those times when you're not present and life is a distraction. This is where practice comes in. You learn methods to bring you back to that experience of awakening, to the end, until the job is complete. After a while, the practice never stops. Of course, from the perspective of enlightenment, the practice itself is not just you practicing but is Source's grace.

I do not want to mislead you. When you wake up in the present, *it really is forever*. And then your *awareness* of it passes. Remember, to be Only Human means that you will lose everything—including your awareness of enlightenment.

> *When you wake up in the present, it really is forever.*

For many of you, once you begin to have these experiences, over time you will have more of them. They will last longer and come more frequently until the present becomes the lens through which you experience your day-to-day life. At any point in this process, some people—perhaps you—will cross over into the present and not come back. But even if that doesn't happen, you can certainly be much more awake and competent.

Through noticing, you *will* regain your natural competence. This competence is not really based on experience, but is spiritually based. It's grounded in that momentary or longer direct connection to Source, when you perceive "what is" exactly as it is.

Someone once asked me if you have to have life experiences to gain competence. Yes, and no matter who you are or how long you've lived, everyone has had a lifetime of experience. The youngest person I've counseled was five years old, and he had spent those five years noticing everything, though he had fewer words or concepts to describe it. Young Sean brought his mother when he came, and he noticed and perceived so much about her that sometimes she couldn't take it. It was difficult for her to handle how much he "knew." He demonstrated phenomenal patience and sensitivity with her, and he was not an out-of-the-ordinary five year old. Children naturally trust what they notice and quickly become competent in many things.

If you wait for the words and concepts to trust your noticing, you'll end up living a life qualified by what you know. Is there anything wrong with spiritual words or concepts? No. Can the words and concepts help? Sure. Are you going to have more experiences in your life for which you don't have adequate words and concepts? Absolutely. Must you wait for the right experiences, the right words, the right concepts in order to wake up in the present forever? No.

No matter how many "personal" experiences you have, together they can never add up to a single experience of everything all at once.

Avocado Consciousness

We all have the ability to wake up in the present forever and taste Avocado Consciousness. With this, you leap into a state of not knowing, where you willingly trade everything you know for an endless instant of not knowing anything in particular. Not knowing is the only way you can avail yourself of knowing everything all at once. That's swallowing the avocado of enlightenment whole.

You can learn to trust those moments when you perceive everything all at once. Whether

The truth is, we've all swallowed the avocado.

it is once a month, once a week, or once a day—every time you do, you end up in that endless moment and open yourself to not recycling what you already know. What you already know has to be some measure of stale, even if you just opened the can. That's why the closest human beings can get to enlightenment is to catch the avocado as it falls. In order to swallow the fruit from the tree, you must become more than Only Human, and there is no description of that. But ordinary human beings can and *do* catch that avocado, straight from Source, that is always falling, always falling. Just suspend your disbelief *and* your belief—and there's the avocado, right in front of you, every time.

In your bones, check it out—will any combination of what you currently know and believe relieve your suffering for long enough? Has it ever? When you even consider abandoning your beliefs for a moment or longer, Avocado Consciousness starts coming in. Then you will be reminded of how perfect it already is, of how whole you already are. The truth is, *we've all swallowed the avocado.*

Chapter 6
The Power of Noticing

As I have said, noticing is having your attention on "what is." When we are noticing, our attention is on reality—what is present to be seen, heard, and felt both inside and outside of us. The power of noticing is how the simple act of noticing exactly "what is" can help us accept our lives, love others, behave competently, and live in an ever-increasing experience of perfection. The natural, organic outcome of noticing is Avocado Consciousness.

When we are not noticing, we will soon feel separated from the world around us even though we are still in the presence of "what is." We feel separated because our attention is on what isn't real. What is the consequence of having your attention on something that isn't in the presence of "what is"? You will attempt to control what is not loved in order to satisfy your preferences. This is the foundation of illusion.

For example, imagine that you pull up to a familiar intersection, the one at which a homeless person is regularly stationed. The light is red and you stop. She has her cardboard sign asking for money or work. Usually, you feel put out or a little put upon by this. Perhaps some mornings you give her a dollar and think and feel whatever you usually think or feel—that the government should do more or that she should get a job, or you speculate about what might have happened to her. Perhaps you're grateful that it's not you.

Just notice how your attention quickly moved from the person on the street ("what is") to your thinking and feeling about the person (usually some version of "what isn't"—how what is should be different).

Noticing and accepting

This morning, let's imagine that you pull up to the intersection and your normal responses don't show up. As you look through the window of your car, you simply notice the other person: the way the light shines through her hair, the shape of her face, the hole in the top of her boot, the brown paper bag resting precariously on her knee, the way the side of the bag has crumpled more on the left than on the right.

This morning, everything you notice, you accept without wanting it to be different—the unwashed hands, the pale skin, the frayed edge of her pants cuff. You feel your hand on the steering wheel and, through it, the vibration of the idling car. Perhaps your window is open enough to hear the morning sounds of the city, so just notice that, too. Let your attention include all of this in a very practical, sensory way.

Congratulations, you're giving effortless attention to "what is," exactly as it is. In noticing her sitting on the sidewalk, you're not wishing she were someone else or someplace else. Your attention is on "what is."

Notice that accepting is not really a second step. When you notice "what is" and stay present with it, without moving to what

Noticing is having your attention on "what is."

you think and feel about it, acceptance is simple and natural—it is just accepting what you notice. Accepting is as simple as not deleting or distorting what you notice.

Appreciation

Deep into this noticing and accepting, this homeless person looks up and sees you noticing her. Do you know what it is she sees? She sees appreciation.

This appreciation has no agenda, no internal dialogue, no "spin." You're not just another politician telling yourself a story. To appreciate the homeless person, you must include all of what you notice. The natural result is that you fall in love with what you notice, and she feels included.

Pure appreciation is also known as unconditional love, or what I like to call unconditioned attention—the currency of human interaction. Every interaction I see between ordinary human beings exchanges attention. Notice me, pay attention.

You can get to pure appreciation without demanding of yourself that you love someone you don't like. Just begin by noticing them and accepting what you notice without deletion or distortion. From where I sit, this is the basis of love: noticing and accepting what you notice, including your own thoughts. When you put noticing and accepting together, you will always find yourself in love with "what is," as it is. You become God's eyes and ears.

Notice that appreciation is not really a third step. Appreciation simply shows up when you accept what you notice. That's why love is so simple and elusive. You can't get there through wanting it. You can't keep it by wanting it to change or be different.

How do you fall out of love? You become selective and only notice the "bad" things. How does love stop growing? You become selective and only notice the "good" things. In either case, you fail to appreciate (notice and accept) the whole of the person, including the so-called "dark side" of people and life situations. This is why I said you can't get to pure appreciation by demanding of yourself that you love someone, or something, or some situation that you don't like. Begin by giving up your preferences for what you like and don't like, and use the power of noticing.

I realize there are few people out there who are demonstrating pure appreciation, so I understand if you aren't sure what it looks like. But to be in the presence of someone who just appreciates you can be life changing. Perhaps you have known one or two people like this in your life—a special grandparent or an influential teacher. What I am suggesting is that there is not an over-supply of such beings. They may do much less in the world of doing. They may not invent new medicines or new explosives. But they are full of noticing, full of acceptance of you, just as you are, with nothing to fix and nothing to change. In fact, you may want to become much more like such a person.

Competence

So how do you become God's hands? How do you know what to do, if anything? This is one of the most asked questions by new students: "OK, so what do I do about—?" If you've ever chewed on that one, just notice that most everything you want to change about yourself, your life situation, other people, or the world is itself the result of doing—and in the case of the world, massive doing.

In New York City before the twentieth century, horse manure was a big problem. The streets were filled with pollution from the horses that took people and goods everywhere. When the "horseless carriage" was invented, it looked like the pollution problem was solved. Of course, one problem was solved but a much larger problem was created. In the world of doing, more doing almost always leads to more problems. With my simple example, I'm not suggesting that you "ignore" problems, or that you do nothing. In fact, from within the lens of doing, doing cannot be avoided. Doing and all

Natural competence is effortless compared to the energy required to control.

of its unintended consequences are wedded to being Only Human and life in the middle. Doing requires that you try to control what is not loved to satisfy your preferences. Noticing, however, leads to a lot less doing. Noticing leads to what I call natural competence.

Let me give you an example of natural competence in action. There is a man who is an excellent computer repair person. Many consider his ability almost uncanny. And boy, does he notice where computers are concerned. In fact, he has no preference for what he notices about computers. I like to say that he has no preference for where the problem is. He is not just a "keyboard" or "hard drive" or "software" person. Unusual problems only seem to spark his curiosity. He simply notices all of the data that comes his way—even information that seems contradictory—and he accepts all of it.

What does all this noticing and accepting demonstrate? What is he demonstrating? Appreciation. It's not too much to say that he loves his work. He now repairs computers so quickly, with so few detours, false starts, or missteps that his colleagues can't quite account for how he does it. He doesn't know how he does it, either. The process is outside of his awareness. The individual steps of noticing, accepting, and appreciating that lead to competence are collapsed into a single step—noticing. It is delightful to watch him at work. He is all awareness.

Welcome to natural competence—doing what needs to be done while doing less and less, simply through the power of noticing. Don't mistake competence for control, however. Control stands the process on its head. Control seeks to change "what is" to satisfy a preference. Control almost always creates a new situation that, soon enough, will require even more effort to "fix it." But natural competence actively rests in a state of noticing and accepting and appreciating. Natural competence is effortless compared to the energy required to control.

Once you master the power of noticing, the process speeds up, and you quickly move from noticing to appreciation of everything around you, including yourself. And you can stop at appreciation—this is what the masters do. To appreciate "what is," as it is, is to love all of God's creation. Of course, if there is anything that needs doing, you'll do it—that's natural competence, that's grace. And you'll do it with immense compassion (appreciation) for the situation and yourself. Why? Because the situation always includes you.

If in any moment you experience confusion or lack of appreciation or acceptance for "what is," then return to noticing. Noticing is not a step you do and go on because you're done with it. Noticing really is the whole ball game—the practice that leads you to Avocado Consciousness and the basis for living a genuinely spiritual life.

Noticing thoughts and feelings

Noticing starts with the senses, but there are many levels on which you can notice. For example, you can notice your thoughts.

There is "what is," and then there's what you think and feel about it—including what you feel and think about what doesn't exist. Thinking about "what isn't" is a kind of illusion, like imagination or daydreaming.

I remember the first time a student noticed the difference between the dirty dishes in the sink and what she thought about them. I asked her, "Do the dishes themselves need washing?" After a longish pause she said, "No." This was the first time in her life that she could remember just noticing the dishes in the sink. She said thinking about the dirty dishes, while not thinking about her need to wash them, hurt her head at first. But she got it—the dirty dishes stacked in the sink were not the cause of her desire to wash them. They were just dirty dishes in the sink.

Try this. If you haven't been able to brush your teeth for a week, do your gritty teeth themselves need brushing? You may "need" to brush them, but they are just being gritty teeth. I'm not suggesting that you stop brushing your teeth, but

Like any good hypnotist, you've come to believe whatever you hear yourself think convincingly.

sometime brush them only because you are brushing them.

It can be liberating to let the messy carpet just be a messy carpet, or to let the dirty dishes just be dirty dishes. After all, these really are external events that do not need to be connected to you by your preferring "what isn't." Remember, noticing in the way I describe always leads to natural competence—doing still gets done, but without the effort control requires.

As you begin to notice the world around you, notice yourself in the world. Your body, including your teeth, is also an external event in the world. Allow your body the same respect and deference to be itself as you would other physical objects—all of which are doing just fine outside of whatever you might think or feel about them.

Consider a physical object that is in the room with you, such as a chair. As something outside of your thinking and feeling, it is an external event. In an obvious way, it is not dependent upon your preferences or opinions about it in order for it to exist in these three dimensions.

As soon as you think about the chair, there is a big shift. While the chair still exists as an external event, for you the thought "chair" has substituted a kind of shorthand for the actual chair. It is now in the realm of thinking and is no longer noticed in these three dimensions. The chair of your thinking and feeling is very different from the actual chair. From my perspective, all "thinking" and all "knowing" takes place in two dimensions; but noticing notices "what is," exactly as it is in three dimensions, apart from your thinking, preferences, and opinions. In fact, noticing is apart from everyone's thinking and feelings.

Notice the chair again. What color is it? Now you may "know" that the chair is green, but did you notice that it isn't green? The actual chair exists in three dimensions, not two. Adding depth, the third dimension, gives the chair texture and highlights and shading—a whole pallet of greens.

When you notice anything or anyone, including yourself, you exit the world of two dimensions. You begin to loosen and lose your opinions, preferences, and judgments. How can you tell when this is happening? The simple presence of something is astounding. Things seem somehow more "real." Colors deepen and become more vibrant; objects may appear to glow from within. You, too, are glowing and vibrant with the same presence, the same realness. Your mind quiets, and you reside in that vast space between thoughts— that alive emptiness out of which all thinking and feeling arise—and you continue to notice.

From that spacious place, you can notice your thinking just as if you were noticing an external event. How? Spaciousness prevents your thoughts and feelings from collapsing onto your body.

Sometimes I suggest to friends and students that they try this exercise in my presence. First, I guide their minds and bodies into that spacious state, where their mind has quieted, their heart has opened, and they are effortlessly listening to the sound of the fan in the room, the bird chirping outside the window. They're noticing all the objects in the room and the space between them, and they're feeling actual sensations in their body, uninterrupted by internal chatter.

Then I suggest that they think about something relatively neutral in their lives, even while they continue to hear the actual sounds around them, see the actual colors and shapes in the room, and feel the actual sensations in their bodies. In other words, their attention is about seventy-five percent on the room and themselves in it and only twenty-five percent on what they're thinking about.

Something really wonderful happens when they do this. The thoughts do not attach to them. It's as if their thinking is not happening in their minds, but happening in the room. Anyone with a little instruction can observe when a person's attention shifts away from the room and over to their thoughts. If you maintain most of your attention in an effortless, relaxed way on the external, thinking is enormously easy. This is why the external is here. When your attention adds up to more than one hundred percent, thinking becomes like noticing—thoughts are fluid and evolving and entertaining. Sometimes I say noticing is thinking after enlightenment.

Almost no one I meet can do this for more than a few seconds by themselves. Part of what makes it possible for people to learn and demonstrate this quickly is that, as a teacher, I am demonstrating the spaciousness. Without word or gesture, I am guiding them again and again into the spacious mind.

When noticing your thoughts, you may need at first to say to yourself or out loud, "There's that thought (again)." I recognize that sometimes students everywhere confuse the internal voice of their thinking ("there's that thought again") with noticing. If you do, you might conclude that noticing is just more thinking, but noticing is not thinking in any ordinary way at all. We are all naturally enlightened because noticing precedes thinking every time, but almost no one's attention is on the noticing. It's all on thinking and feeling.

The confusion between noticing and thinking happens because everyone is suggestible to the sound of their voice commenting in their head. Like any good hypnotist, you've come to believe whatever you hear yourself think convincingly. But noticing "what is," as it is, does not require any auditory confirmation. In fact, noticing will convince you once and for all that you are not the voice in your head.

Face it—your thinking can often be a tyrant. But noticing your thoughts in the way I'm describing, with the same attention and integrity you can learn to give three-dimensional objects, will free you from this tyranny. How? By allowing you to notice this amazing world we live in—which includes the whole of you and all of your thoughts and feelings.

As I said, "thinking" itself exists as a kind of external event, just like physical objects. How? It is actually easier to demonstrate this than to describe it. We have learned that when someone recalls a vivid memory, the memory has many specific qualities including "location."

For example, a vivid memory is usually in color and is relatively "close" to a person. I will say, "Where is this picture located? Show me with your hand and arm." If she hesitates I add, "Now I know that it isn't twenty feet above your head or forty feet behind you. Just let your hand show me." And she will, every time. The person might say, "It's right here," and hold her hand two feet in front of her at chest level.

When she recalls an indistinct memory, it is often a "small" picture, perhaps fuzzy and in black and white, and she will indicate that it is farther away from her, perhaps twelve feet away and at floor level. We have learned that when something is "in your face" and making you a little crazy, your thinking and feeling is literally "in your face"—that is the location. In fact, from the perspective of noticing, very few thoughts are actually located inside your head.

Remember the exercise on noticing your thoughts as external events? When practicing this, notice that your memories and thinking could be found on a three-dimensional grid around your body, with each thought having a specific elevation and distance from you, just like physical objects. Now you may remember or think more in sounds than in pictures, but these sounds also have specific qualities, including location.

Many times I know where the person's memory or picture is located, and so do others, mostly outside of their awareness. Often I "see" their internal pictures and "hear" their internal conversations. Do I try to do this? No. This ability just showed up as a consequence of noticing.

How is it possible to see and hear others' thoughts? I don't really know. But it makes more sense when you realize that our thinking is a kind of external event, just like physical objects. If you want to, you can speculate that this may be the basis for many psychic phenomena. In any case, as you learn to notice, you are in for many delightful surprises.

Perfection

Many years ago, I had a practice of just sitting in the living room all day, every day. No reading, or writing, or watching TV, or meditating. I got my wife off to work and the kids delivered to school. Then I returned home and sat on the floor or couch or chair. Our two indoor rabbits and two cats entertained me sometimes, but mostly they just ignored me. I did this for over eight weeks.

On one particular day, I "woke up." I began to notice the ordinary items in the room—chair, picture frame, wall clock. They looked different—substantially different. The colors were heightened, and everything was delightfully three-dimensional. For the first time, I really noticed how they all occupied space. It occurred to me, "So this is living in three dimensions." I had discovered the actual world.

As I looked around, my eyes settled on our couch. This was the couch that I had just paid a thousand dollars for and my wife's cat was already shredding. She thought it was cute and hopeless to change, while I fumed about it. On this day, however, I discovered I was neutral—no, it was more than neutral. My preference for the couch to not be shredded was gone. The couch looked perfect just as it was. Or rather, what was true was that the couch was clawed, and—reality being "what is"—it was also perfect.

I felt light and solid, at ease and aware. As I looked around the room, everything was glowing from within, heightening the colors. It was all perfect just as it was. Then I happened to look down at my body. Here I was, also in the room, glowing from within, the body just being itself. There was nothing to fix or change, nothing about me that needed improving. I discovered that my body is an external event, too. "So this is perfection," I thought, and it is perfectly normal. My teachers described enlightened mind as "ordinary mind." I then understood that it takes some extra-ordinariness to realize this.

There's no point in writing about perfection with an exclamation point. The exclamations only show up as you enter perfection or after you've left. It is the contrast between your "everyday" life and these non-personal experiences that creates the exclamation. In an experience of "perfection," everything is revealed in its natural context, including every aspect of your life, just as it is, quite natural.

During my awakening, I spontaneously began to lucid dream and astral travel. At the beginning of each of these experiences, there was a moment and longer when I experienced the perfection of everything, and then I went on to have a dream that was exciting or healing or spiritual. For a long time, I did not understand that the fruit of all of these experiences was not what was obviously exciting or healing or spiritual; rather, the fruit was that moment of perfection.

The self-demonstration of perfection is the only teaching.

I could say that when your attention is on perfection, you disappear and all that remains is perfection. This is what it means to have "your" attention on "what is." With anything less, your attention becomes unevenly divided. For most of us, most of the time, our attention is on what doesn't exist. What is the effect of investing your attention on "what isn't" in the presence of "what is"? Most of human suffering—and most of your suffering—is the result of just this.

"What is," exactly as it is, is all of God's creation. All the possibilities of what can be, but is not yet, are contained in and will be expressed through "what is." *To understand "what is," is to understand all possibilities.* This is the rapture of appreciation for "what is," as it is, and as it will be.

"What is," as it is, is the present. What else could it be?

All new possibilities are expressed in the present. When else could they be?

Using the materials—the stuff at hand—to express a new possibility uses only what exists in the present. What else could be used?

The flip side of noticing

Once again, noticing is having your attention on "what is." When we are noticing, our attention is on reality—what is present to be seen, heard, and felt both inside and outside of us. The simple act of noticing *exactly* what is can help us accept our lives, love others, behave competently, and live in an ever-increasing experience of perfection. This is the natural, organic outcome of noticing.

As the chart on the next page shows, what almost everyone does is stand reality—"what is"—on its head. Then you appear to no longer receive the support that reality is always providing. Separation

Noticing and its Opposites

What is–Reality

*Perceiving the wholeness–
life is complete in this
moment and longer*

What isn't–Illusion

*Everything is in process–
imcomplete. Life comes
in pieces and parts*

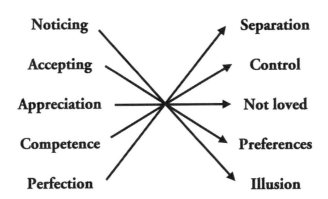

Noticing	Separation
Accepting	Control
Appreciation	Not loved
Competence	Preferences
Perfection	Illusion

replaces perfection. When we are *not* noticing, we will soon *feel* separated from the world around us, even though we are still in the presence of "what is." We feel separated because our attention is on what isn't real.

When we start from a place of *separation*, we all try to *control* (or manage, or direct, or facilitate—pick what ever doing verb you prefer) what is *not loved* to satisfy our *preferences* and stay in *illusion*. We've cast our vote for "what isn't" and reinforce living in confusion with the suffering that naturally follows. In other words, you have stopped noticing. Rather than having an experience of perfection, you experience separation, where everything seems to need an overhaul, or at least a fine-tuning. This is why separation (with its suffering) is the opposite and complement of perfection.

The opposite and complement of competence is *control*. Control brings force to change "what is" because we don't like it. Control is the opposite of God's grace; competence comes from God's grace. Competence comes from giving and receiving the support reality is always offering.

The opposite and complement of appreciation is *not loved*. You cannot simultaneously appreciate an individual or life situation and not love it. Loving it does not mean that you condone or approve of what is there. The appreciation I'm talking about is "spiritual" love and it is as simple as I am suggesting.

The opposite and complement of accepting is *preferences*. With preference, there is no pause of acceptance. With preference we immediately move to our thinking and feeling, which will always soon enough say yes or no, right or wrong, good or bad, I like it or I don't like it.

And finally, the opposite and complement of noticing is *illusion*. With our illusions intact, we remain unknowingly committed to our life in the middle, continually recycling our personal and cultural illusions.

Why is each of these not only the opposite but also the complement of the other? Because, from my perspective, this illusion-making—this state of separation—*is also* God's setup for us. Doesn't it have to be? It's not too much to say that this illusion is also "what is."

Am I suggesting that you give up all of your preferences or your need to control all at once? Being Only Human, that's not possible. But you can begin by practicing noticing for sixty seconds twice a day. You can sit in your living room, eyes open, and want the room to be exactly the way it is: the pillow just that shade of blue, the carpet slightly askew, your children's toys scattered exactly where they are and not two inches to the left. At first, notice only what you can sense. Do not yet shift your attention to anything that cannot be seen or heard or smelled or tasted or physically sensed right around you. This helps to keep your attention on "what is."

Soon enough, you'll be up to five minutes a day. Now you are noticing what is actually present. It's amazing what begins to happen. You get to exit life in the middle—it really is that simple. Your moment-to-moment experience is no longer a recycling of any previous experience. Your natural clarity of appreciation does not require that you try to control what God has created. When you experience God's actual sounds, sights, and sensations, you fall in love with all of it and all of us and all of every life situation. From my perspective, this is what it means to live and act from love. If your love is not expressed from these three dimensions, it is usually, at best, just a good idea.

How many times a day do people try to control themselves and what's around them? Lots and lots. Every time you try to control something, you are demonstrating that it is unloved by you. You have separated yourself from God's creation; you are arguing with the universe. Why would any of us go through most of our hours doing this? Because this is what our separation demands. Noticing demonstrates exactly the opposite. Noticing requires that you notice exactly "what is" without distorting or deleting anything. This noticing and acceptance of "what is" undoes the separation and returns us to perfection.

How pervasive is illusion? How many times a day do you try to control what you don't love in order to satisfy a preference? Can you even consider how it affects your emotional life to have an ongoing perception of events, people, and activities as not exactly the way you want them?

When words get in the way of enlightenment

Will words and concepts get in the way? Absolutely. The words and concepts get in the way *all the time*. Do you realize that we only have words and concepts for a fraction of what is available to experience? The fact that writers and storytellers have been telling the same stories in different forms for thousands of years, from my perspective, just demonstrates that human beings are stuck—stuck with the same few experiences. We're recycling through the same stories, the same dozen dramas, comedies, and intrigues—*the same dozen emotions*—over and over again. Listen to any newscast, pick up any book: love, betrayal, guilt, revenge, jealousy, heroism, sacrifice, again and again. From my perspective, that's stuck, and that's Only Human, isn't it?

Words and concepts can only describe what is there to be noticed. Living in grace does not require that you have the words or concepts to describe living in grace. Teaching and guiding others doesn't require that you have the words or concepts, either, although it helps. Sometimes I use these words and concepts as a kind of mind candy to describe, from our own perspective, being Only Human and more. If you're reading these words, what I'm demonstrating has almost nothing to do with the words and ideas, the sentences and phrases. It has almost everything to do with the ink on the paper, the sensation in your hands, the weight of the book. This demonstrates the whole universe.

This is the power of noticing—to notice and accept how much time you spend in memories and associations, comparing and contrasting, planning and fantasizing. When you accept and appreciate this, you get a glimpse of what is actually here—the sheer perfection of it all, which has nothing to do with what you normally think and feel.

When you glimpse the three-dimensional world and accept and appreciate exactly what is here, does this three-dimensional world include you? Of course! Yes! You are a perfect demonstration of this perfection. The appreciation that follows from this is not just personal. It will never fit into any personal experience. You don't need words and concepts to experience this appreciation. Through this noticing and accepting and appreciating, you will effortlessly demonstrate perfection. *This self-demonstration of perfection is the only teaching.* That is all that is ever demonstrated. That is all that I'm leading you to again, and again, and again. It is the end of all your questions and the beginning of living in grace.

When questions end

Having revealed the secret of the universe, the man in the back of the room has a question. Turns out, it's a great question. It's a question that deserves an answer. He's a human being, sincere and honest and loving, and he deserves an answer, too. So I will offer him a description of his world, and your world, that mirrors his personal experience *and more*. I will offer distinctions and discernments and a discussion that will open the door of his question until he has no more doors or questions that need opening. When will his questions come to an end? His questions will end when he no longer has any objections to living in the present.

Are these distinctions and discernments that I am offering accurate? Are they *real*? Yes, of course, and they are completely arbitrary. The universe will allow itself to be divided and classified and categorized in an *infinite* number of ways. It is also demonstrating the corollary, complement, and opposite of each distinction. That's how compassionate the universe is.

Chapter 7
A Conversation on Noticing

The dialogue in this chapter was taken from a talk on noticing. When I work with people in groups, I lead them into the state of noticing. As I talk, I also *demonstrate* each step until the listeners also demonstrate their understanding—even if they are unaware of it. No words or gestures are required for them to demonstrate their understanding. From my perspective, actual spirituality can be enormously subtle.

Demonstrating has nothing to do with the intellect or thinking or even feeling. A child demonstrates his "understanding" of crawling by crawling. A bird demonstrates its understanding of flying by flying. This *understanding* of crawling and flying can only be demonstrated in these three dimensions. Everything else is just talk.

From life in the middle, it is very difficult to notice what is being demonstrated by the world and yourself, so real understanding is rare. Mostly, what passes for noticing is just more of what you think and feel. But you *can* notice what you and others demonstrate in the same way you can notice what a child or a bird or a concrete slab demonstrates. With a genuine experience of spiritual awakening, you move on to the beginning, where it becomes much easier to gain this real understanding. After you get it—that noticing has almost nothing to do with your judgments, opinions, or preferences or anyone else's—it can be painfully clear how easy it is to fool ourselves.

Noticing in three dimensions

People sometimes say, "I agree. Objective reality isn't the problem; the problem is the thinking in my head." So let me ask you: if the thinking is in your head, where is your head? I think your head is in the room. I think it's right next to the back of the chair where you're sitting. In this way—and this way *only*—your problems *are* part of reality. You don't ever really leave three dimensions, even when you experience other "spiritual" dimensions. And a lot of the work that we do with people is about returning them to what I call "these three dimensions."

So I'll give you a demonstration of three dimensions. What color is my shirt?

Q. Light tan.

Light tan. So right between reality and illusion, we have knowing and its cousin, thinking. So you might know that my shirt is tan. But in three dimensions, it is not tan. In these three dimensions, there's height, there's width—what's the third dimension?

Q. Depth.

Depth. Now look at my shirt, and notice what depth does for my shirt.

Q. Ok. I notice gray in it.

Yes. It's darker there, and it's lighter here. It has a nice burnish of light over here. It's much lighter there. My shirt is a whole palette of whites and tans.

Whatever I say will make perfect sense if you notice, as you sit there, the actual colors in my shirt and the actual colors of other objects in the room. Also include the sounds in the room and sensations in your body. Notice the shading of light on the walls. Listen to the refrigerator in the kitchen and the bird outside. Feel your actual physical sensations—the way your feet feel resting on the floor, the way your arm is cooler outside your sleeve and warmer under your sleeve.

All of this can be noticed. I call it noticing "what is." Why would you want to notice what is? Because "what is" is reality, apart from anything that's going on in your head or emotions, apart from everything that you would normally think and feel. This thinking includes the conversations in your head—you know, the voice in your head. How many of you thought, "What voice in my head?" *That* voice.

When you have your attention on the actual sounds you hear and on what you actually see, all you have to do next is *accept* what you are noticing. Accept that the chair is just that far from the wall. Accept that the fabric is just that shade of red. Acceptance is just accepting what you notice, exactly as it is. Always begin noticing with the senses, begin in three dimensions. Acceptance is as simple as not wishing my hair were blonde, or I was five years younger, or I was six inches closer to you.

You can notice, even though you don't have a tape measure, how close I am to you. You can notice the actual sounds in the room. When your attention is on the actual sounds, the actual sensations, what you actually see—light, form, texture—you support reality. It's that simple.

When you're just noticing how things actually are, you also support Source or God or the universe. When your attention is on what you can actually notice in these three dimensions, you support Source's will. Aligning your will with Source is just that close. Whoever knew it was that close? It doesn't take much work at all. So I ask, in this moment, how does Source, or God, want the world to be?

Q. Well, according to what you're saying, exactly as it is.

Exactly as it is. Even though you may not understand it.

You can align your will with God's will if your attention is on how everything is and you accept what you notice. Acceptance is as simple as not wishing that anything in the room be different. You can do this noticing and accepting even while thinking about war or starving children.

What people do is they get themselves in situations where they think about events that they really have no influence on in this moment. In that way, they abandon everyone and everything actually around them. How do people get lost in their thinking? They leave these three dimensions, and all of their attention goes elsewhere.

Of course, reality is not just what you sense in your immediate environment. If you want to think about something that's not within your senses, do so. Just keep at least half of your attention also on your surroundings. In this way, you actively support God's creation, even while you wonder if there's anything for *you* to do to change the situation in the Middle East.

From this place in this room today, what can *you* do about war? A reasonable response might be, "I don't know." Or maybe you get that there isn't anything for you to do. And maybe you get there *is* something for you to do, but is this something just an automatic response based on your preferences? Or does this something follow from a direct appreciation of the whole of the human situation and more?

As far as I can tell, the source of all human suffering is having your attention on "what isn't" in the presence of "what is." Potential suffering is as easy as wishing I were older or ten feet away from you, or your chair were a little further back or a little softer, or your eyes were blue and not green. See how easy it is to abandon reality? And where is your attention when it's on "what isn't"? It's on an illusion. Your attention is on what doesn't exist. When you abandon the way things are, when you abandon the support reality or Source provides, you will experience pain every time.

> *The source of all human suffering is having your attention on "what isn't" in the presence of "what is."*

This is a perfectly normal and ordinary and foolish pain. When we prefer our opinions and judgments about what is, rather than just notice what is, we fool ourselves.

I get to watch human beings interact all the time. Often they delete and distort what it is they notice about someone else, especially someone that they don't like. They just don't want to hear or see anything that would have them empathize with the other person. The only way they can do this is to start filtering anything they find agreeable. Soon enough, they have left these three dimensions. They've left God's creation. I can't believe sometimes how fast people abandon reality.

Remember, thinking is always in two dimensions. Noticing is always three dimensions.

So when you look at the shirt, you think "tan." After a while, this thought becomes a kind of shorthand that gets used everywhere. Consider all the people you know. When they see you, they think to themselves, "Oh yeah, there's Karen." And then they move on. They no longer notice you. Are you ready for a revolutionary idea? The actual Karen is the one in three dimensions. But most of your friends don't see the actual Karen. Oh, they notice you all right, but their noticing is almost instantaneously given over to everything they think and know about you. And now "Karen" is really just a kind of shorthand that stands in for you, just like the shorthand that stands in for this actual shirt. The problem is that this shorthand can only be in two dimensions—there's no reality to it. All of Source's creation is missed—the whole incredible palette of colors, the richness of the actual sounds, and the actual human beings that stand before you.

Sometimes I sit in this chair for hours a day—not meditating, not sleeping, not spacing out—just here. I've discovered that by being in these three dimensions, when someone comes through the room, I get to notice the *actual* person. I get to notice all the subtleties of how they move, walk, changes in breath, skin tone, eye dilation, slump of the shoulders. And because I have no preference for what I notice, I get to know all kinds of things about them.

When you notice in the way I'm describing, and you simply accept without preference what you notice, you will automatically *appreciate* what you notice. This is *loving "what is,"* just as it is. When you notice, you automatically fall in love with what you notice. I fall in love all day long.

So I sit and I get to notice actual human beings—the way the light is brighter on one side of your face and a little darker on the other side, the way the light comes through your hair, a whole palette of colors on your clothes, the form and texture of your body.

Early on when I noticed in this way, I'd have these experiences of waking up in the present and I'd say, "Oh my God, everything is so three-dimensional!" All the colors were so heightened. It's that way for me all the time now. When I look at the flowers on the porch over there, there's no conversation in my head about the flowers, so there's nothing standing between me and perceiving directly the incredible colors of the petals—or perceiving a piece of concrete rubble or the way a cat moves or a bug jumps or a child sneezes.

The life of the IMP

As far as I can tell, most people don't experience these three dimensions. Rather, they experience the shorthand I talked about earlier. I call this the IMP—an Instantaneous Memory of the Present. Of course they do notice and experience this actual present that I'm talking about, but it quickly passes. It may be that their experience of the present moves directly to that part of the brain where memories and associations reside.

You cannot talk about or compare anything in the present without shifting into a memory of the present. That may be why, whatever their experience is, people can immediately talk about it, justify it, defend it, and explain it. Direct experience, however, cannot be analyzed, compared, or explained because direct experience is never *like* anything else.

I imagine that as a little kid, you were sitting out there playing in the mud, and your mother came out and said, "What are you doing?"

What were you doing? Of course, you weren't "doing" anything. There was just form and texture and goo and all those sensations. She may have said, "You've made a mess," and you may have been scolded or punished for "making a mess." Soon enough, you learned to offer explanations for what you were doing. With the right explanation, you would be left alone or even rewarded. What was it that was being demonstrated to you?

You had to leave these three dimensions and, with an instantaneous shift of your attention, activate those parts of the brain that would allow you to recognize, "This is like some other experience." So now you could say to your mother, "Oh, this is what I'm doing." Now you could offer up good reasons and reasonable excuses.

No combination of miracles by themselves will bring you to spiritual maturity.

When you shift your attention out of the present, you instantly make a copy of the present. This copy becomes a memory that can be compared to all your other memories of the present. Meanwhile, the actual present is still *right there with you*, but your attention is not on it. Your attention is on the copy.

For almost all human beings, this copy is produced so fast and so smoothly that you don't notice the *bump*. As you learn to notice when your attention shifts out of the present, you will experience this bump as a BIG bump in your consciousness. Hundreds of millions of times, everyone around us has demonstrated, "Ignore the bump! Ignore the bump!" It's like hitting one of those speed bumps at ninety miles per hour. You leave the ground! You are airborne! Of course, everyone around you is saying, "What bump?" So you believe you didn't. Spiritual teachers are here to remind you—emphatically—that you did!

Kids learn really fast how to ignore the bump and offer up explanations, give great justifications, and analyze everything. Bang, bang, bang—they leave the present. Everything becomes shorthand for their direct experience. Their whole lives become shorthand. The IMP basically lives your life for you.

All of your memories and associations are useful and can be entertaining, but they cannot be substituted for the direct experience of reality. To experience three-dimensional reality and not your "ideas" of all of it—including your ideas of yourself—you have to notice first with your senses and then discover how quickly the actual present is given over to this facsimile of the present.

Although the IMP operates simultaneously with the actual present, it's still behind your act of noticing. The good news is the IMP can never get ahead of noticing. Source provided you with an ability to notice that cannot be taken away. This noticing precedes *every* thought and feeling. This is why sometimes I say, "Awakening is closer than your next thought."

Staying out of the principal's office

So notice the actual sounds in the room. Contained in the sounds are volume, tone, tempo, cadence, and pitch. Hear how rich those sounds are? That's why musicians can live such incredible lives, at least some of them, because they can hear all of that. This is the way artists see things. They can paint a chair and you'd say it's alive.

To be like a musician or artist, all you have to do is *notice* "what is," beginning with these three dimensions, and *accept* what you notice without wishing anything were different, which automatically leads to *appreciating* what you notice. You can fall in love with anything by appreciating it exactly as it is. From that place, you'll get to know what, if anything, there is for you to do about something. That's *competence*—and it has nothing to do with thinking, nothing to do with what you know, nothing to do with principles, or morals, or beliefs. I sometimes say that we don't need very many principles, which is good news, because eventually your principles will spank you.

As competence flows from appreciation, you may get to know what it is you are to do next. If you do, say "thank you." But remember, knowing what to do slows the whole process down. Noticing is very fast, very fluid. When noticing begins to slow down, you get to know something. We all appreciate those "ah-ha" moments, when we have a flash of insight or sudden knowing. So say "thank you," and let them go.

If knowing itself slows down, the whole process starts to thicken. Life gets sticky. Knowing becomes belief. The whole point of owning a belief is that you no longer have to be present when the future arrives. You believe you can rely on principles to guide you. Why would you need them to guide you? Because you are no longer in the present.

The same is true of rules. I find it fascinating the way we all hold on to rules. Most everyone will resist examining the rules and vigorously defend any existing rules. Why? They are hoping this will make the future predictable. But since you only ever experience the present—only ever live in the present—rules won't work for long.

People say to me, "Teach me the rules of—." Pick something: relationships, career, money, spiritual development. So I explain culture's setup for those things, and then they go out and play. After a few hours, or a few years, they come back a little bruised and say, "Teach me the exceptions to the rules." So I teach them the exceptions. Of course, they return again. "Wait," they say, "this is more complicated than I thought. Teach me the rules of how to apply the exceptions." If I continued playing this game, they would be back again and again, requesting more exceptions and more rules.

From my perspective, this seems like a lot of work and a lot of trouble. They want to know what the rules are to predict how to behave in the future. But I repeat, you only ever experience the present. So while your attention is on the rules and the future, you miss what's in the present—what is actually here and how it expresses itself. Better to notice the present, demonstrate competence, and live in perfection. Noticing is an economical, energy-saving affair.

Genuine spiritual work is not about knowing more, but along the way you will know more about yourself and the world around you. As noticing becomes easier, you naturally give up everything you know in favor of everything you don't know. Don't worry—there is no end to what you can know. Trying to hang on to knowing is inefficient and troublesome. Soon enough, today's brilliant insight becomes tomorrow's stale explanation. What keeps the juice in the juicy fruit of knowing is noticing.

In the present, beliefs and principles and moral teachings are effortlessly self-demonstrated by the universe and everything in it, but they don't show up as something broad and flat and fixed, which must be interpreted or blindly followed in each particular situation. Rather, they are fresh and obvious and effortlessly tailored, right here, right now—ahhhh—and so you turn left instead of right. No internal debates; no federal committees.

Living in grace

To practice noticing, I recommend people hang out with the actual stuff around them for sixty seconds in the morning and sixty seconds in the evening, to begin with. You might want to start out somewhere in the woods, or in the quiet in your home when there's nobody there. Start by just noticing how things actually are. By that I mean notice the elevation of objects, notice how far apart objects are from each other, become aware of the space between objects, notice the actual colors, the actual sounds. And as you notice, accept everything you notice just as it is, without deleting or distorting any of it. When you do that, you become God's eyes and ears. Everybody breathes easier.

That's why people go out in nature. When you go out to the state park, there's no voice in your head saying, "You know, this plant needs transplanting and that plant needs pruning and someone should weed over there and that tree ought to be another color...." But it's typically not that way when you're in your home. It seems there's all this stuff you have to do.

From a place of noticing, you'll discover there's a whole lot less to do than you ever thought there was. I call this natural competence. Natural competence is about doing what needs to be done with fewer false starts, missteps, and detours. It's not a question of what *needs* doing; it's a question of, "From *this* place, what in *this* moment do you actually do about anything in this room?" This is living in grace.

Practice your natural competence, and it will lead right into *perfection*, the last step in the dance of noticing. I remember the first time Jenée got to notice that the dishes *themselves* didn't need washing. They were already done, complete, whole. The carpet itself didn't need vacuuming. You get it? *The whole world is done.* It may not meet your preferences. You may think that the carpet needs vacuuming, or it doesn't need vacuuming. You may prefer it to be one way or the other. But the carpet *itself* is done. This is when you step out of personal preferences and begin to live in perfection.

From my perspective, spiritual madness is overrated.

Now, can you hang out there for hours and days? Maybe, but probably not. I remember Astrid one day said, "Oh that's fine, but if it's true that everything in the universe is already done, then what's stopping me from sitting on the couch all day?" I said, "Try it! We both know what will happen. You'll sit there for maybe twenty minutes, and then it'll be like you're spring-loaded and you'll pop up because, you know, you've got things to do!" She just laughed and laughed. There's not a chance she'll sit around in perfection all day.

From this place of noticing and discovering your own natural competencies, you may discover that there are other things for you to do, things you may not have considered. You may become a spiritual teacher; it's entirely possible. I like to say sometimes that there's a lot of room at the top. You know, there are not too many people out there appreciating other human beings for exactly how they show up. That could be a great career move for you.

Now and then, I work with people who are dying, who have lost a child, or have lost a career. You should see what happens when for just thirty seconds they notice how it is and they want it to be just the way it is. You see them relax. It lets so much pressure off of them because from that place they'll discover what, if anything, there is to do about the situation, and they'll do it with competence.

So now, just for thirty seconds, notice the lighting on Jenée's face, the highlights and the shadows around her eyes, under her chin. If we went out to a restaurant and Jenée's face had this same lighting on it, wouldn't it be so strange? If we went outside and her face still had the same shadows while standing in bright sunlight, we would say, "Jenée, what happened to your face?" But in fact, that's what her face looks like *right now*. You see what I'm talking about? That's what's actually here to be seen, without deleting or distorting, without any shorthand.

Further, by noticing and seeing what's actually here to be seen, and hearing what's actually here to be heard, from that place, you can ask, "So what do I do about—" and fill in the blank. You can consider, "Is there anything specific for me to do about something that concerns me?" When you ask the question, keep noticing and *don't let your attention leave the room.* Your attention stays here. Let what is not quite in your visual awareness—what's not quite seen—let it be not quite seen from *here.* Let what is not quite heard or understood be not quite heard from *here.* If your luck is mixed, you may get a specific answer from the universe. In other words, you may get to know what it is you are to do. If you're really lucky, you won't have to know. You'll just find yourself doing it. As I said, this is living in grace.

Restoring context

One of the things I've discovered along the way is that anyone can learn to sit and ask, with eyes open, a simple question like, "What about one of my friends, like Avril in Canada? What about Tim in Atlanta?" You could learn about them while sitting and staying present. You can learn quite a lot about friends in distant places if you don't leave your present surroundings.

If the question concerning you is, "Should I move to that little apartment in Denver and go to community college in the spring," it's too specific of a question. What you have created is a very small context. It's more useful to ask a question about the larger context.

Ask instead, "What about college?" Later you can ask, "What about Denver?" That allows your whole life situation to be the context. Then whether or not to rent that apartment will easily find its place in the larger context of your life. You will see how the smaller pieces fit into the rest of your life.

If your concern is how do I pay the electric bill by Tuesday, again it's a very specific question. If not paying bills on time is an ongoing or emerging pattern for you, you need to ask a larger question, such as, "What about money?" That way, the context or map you're creating will include everything about you and money, including how to pay the electric bill by Tuesday. The larger context becomes a kind of constantly updated map of your whole life—a much bigger perspective than simply the crossroads that you are standing in. This larger perspective always brings peace of mind because let's face it—this time you may not get the electric bill paid by Tuesday. You will not be able to meet everyone's expectations of you. You will disappoint other people, just as surely as they will disappoint you. Why let any of that make you crazy?

When asking "what about," I sometimes encourage people to get no data at all. If I have a preference for what I learn, a preference for what comes through, a preference for the miraculous over the ordinary, it slows the process way, way down. The old Zen saying is true: "Not knowing means there's nothing that is not known."

Sometimes when you get data, you have an experience that can leave you shaken for some period of time. This data might include a vision, either inside your mind or outside your body, what I sometimes call a "true hallucination." Or you may hear sounds that could include the voice of an angel or guide or perhaps celestial music. In an important way, these experiences are part of the fruit of spiritual practice. But like any fruit, it has a limited shelf life. Soon enough you're left with only memories. For many people, they're left not only with memories of these experiences but also with real trauma. These experiences can shake people and leave them shaken for a long time. Ordinary people unprepared for spiritual experiences can find themselves in therapy for hearing voices or seeing visions. For those of you expecting spiritual experiences, having them may not be progress. For now, let me say that spiritual experiences sometimes can serve to move us forward on our journey, but often these experiences become a very real kind of distraction.

For almost everyone on the journey, these experiences also will become a kind of baggage—a collection of possessions to be reminisced and romanced and sorted through and catalogued and compared to your friends' collections. Soon enough, a very real experience has been stuffed and mounted, a kind of trophy. Do not become a taxidermist of your own life.

All of these experiences become something that you must let go of, as surely as you must let go of any other experience you've had.

Why must you let go of it? Because the experience has passed.

When I encourage people to get no data at all, I am suggesting they bring these pictures, sounds, and physical sensations to the edge of their awareness, to the edge of their presence, without having them intrude. Or perhaps they can allow them into their awareness without losing the three-dimensional awareness of everything else around them. In this way, you don't have to process yet another big experience in your life.

This is an important training. Then when an angel or guide appears to you, or a bowl of Cheerios materializes right on the kitchen table just as you think of it, say "thank you" to all of that. Enjoy the Cheerios. Enjoy hearing from your guide. Then let them go. Do not become possessed of any of that, including the miraculous bowl of Cheerios. Keep fifty to seventy-five percent of your attention on the other actual sounds in the room, on the form and texture of everything else that you see and feel, including the table the bowl is sitting on. Why? Because none of these experiences can live your life for you, whether it is an experience of the miraculous or an experience of the ordinary.

No combination of miracles by themselves will bring you spiritual maturity. Isn't that interesting? I listen to people who have the most amazing spiritual experiences, and almost to a person, none of those experiences brought them one measure of spiritual maturity.

When you meet someone who has spiritual maturity, they will say of their spiritual life, "Yes, there is that," and you get that it is not something they talk a lot about or make a big deal out of. They are not possessed by the experience. From my perspective, spiritual madness is overrated.

Just let the data come, and let it go. Soon enough, you will reside in that place from which both the miraculous and the ordinary dwell—that place that is always here, right here, right now. How did that which is always whole get split into the ordinary and the miraculous? It only got split in our thinking and feeling. Our thinking and feeling have a role in our journey but also create spiritual mischief.

What are we demonstrating?

So from the present—and I'll say right up front that I avoid when I can using the words *present, consciousness, unconscious, awareness,* or *higher self.* Well, there might be a few times, but not often because culture has acquired these words and the human beings who use them. That means the listener may nod her head and say or think to herself, "Yes, I understand what you're saying; perhaps I even agree with you." But is the listener *demonstrating* what she believes she understands?

From where I stand, people are remarkably honest. When Karen nods her head, she believes that she does understand what I'm saying.

It is not as if she is trying to mislead me or herself. I can observe that she understands the "words," but is she demonstrating the experience that the words point to? If not, then she is substituting the words for the experience, and her understanding is only intellectual. Now, intellectual understanding is fine as far as it goes. It's just that the intellect never goes very far—it certainly never goes all the way. It's like collecting baseball cards of your perfect romantic date but never actually going out, much less sleeping over.

This is what culture does. Culture, even "alternative culture," teaches you to get the words right and "communicate" with others. If this actually worked, why is there so much miscommunication and hurt feelings?

You can't always trust what someone says—all their words are just what they say—but you can always trust what they demonstrate.

> *Not noticing what you demonstrate is how you fool yourself.*

So someone says to me, "Got it Steve," and I observe them. If they demonstrate what they understand right in the moment, I respond with "Yes! You do have it." If they are *not* demonstrating it, then I must say "no" so as to not mislead them.

This can be very interesting when one person says to me, "Are you talking about the present?" And I say, "No." The very next person says, "But you must be talking about the present." And I say, "Yes." Why would I do this? Because I will only respond to what you demonstrate. If you are in the present when you say "present" then yes, if not, then no. To do anything less would just make your life more difficult.

In my teaching, I keep encouraging human beings, directing them to notice what they're actually demonstrating and what other human beings are actually demonstrating.

Q. Is demonstrating the same as "doing"?

Maybe! Did you notice that she just demonstrated "doing," earning her a "maybe"? Why not a "yes"? Because doing is not the same as demonstrating, but it is closer than just words. How about a relatively obvious example:

Jenée, please say to Karen that you love her and that you want to spend the rest of your life with her.

Q. I love you and I want to spend the rest of my life with you. (She laughs.)

So, does Jenée really love Karen and want to spend the rest of her life with her? Jenée's response was probably not a hundred percent yes or a hundred percent no, but somewhere in the middle. What did you notice? Was it fifty percent yes, fifty percent no? Eighty percent yes, twenty percent no? Twenty percent yes, eighty percent no?

Do you see how much trouble people get into because they

hear the words "I love you and want to spend the rest of my life with you" or "I want to have your child" or "Of course I'll support you if you move all the way across the country" or "All I need is half your savings and my business will succeed and then we'll get married"?

They say the right words. What happens is that the listener (and that includes all of you) stops noticing what the other human being is actually demonstrating. See, it has nothing to do with the words. Clearly, Jenée doesn't really want to spend the rest of her life with Karen, at least not at this time, even though she was smiling and giggling. We know it was probably about a twenty percent "yes," eighty percent "no." All of that can be noticed—the percent of "no" in the yes, and the percent of "yes" in the no.

This is an example of what a human being actually demonstrates apart from the words they use. With any group of people, I can teach them to accurately notice these percentages of yes and no in just a few minutes, even though they may have no idea how they are able to notice. Can you appreciate how much easier life would become if you were not fooled by the words?

Great actors, con men, and politicians are able to help you fool yourself by supporting your preference for what they are saying to be true. That's how someone fools you with words.

Have you ever told a lover that you never wanted to see them again, yet they kept returning again and again, with notes and phone calls and messages? Why didn't they go away? Could it be that they noticed the ten or twenty or thirty percent "yes" every time you said "no"?

When you begin to accurately notice what *you* demonstrate, apart from what you think and feel and say, life will get much easier. Not noticing what you demonstrate is how you fool yourself.

Levels of perception

Demonstrating is what is revealed by every object, individual, and life or cultural situation apart from what you normally think and feel. We cannot *not* demonstrate "what is," though we've learned to ignore what we demonstrate and believe instead what someone says or does. In collusion, we agree to not notice and say, "I'll believe who you think you are if you believe who I think I am."

Viewed from within our consensual illusion, there seems to be levels of noticing what is demonstrated. These levels begin with life in the middle, where everything seems to be about what we think and feel and do.

On the first level, almost nothing is really noticed just as it is. This is Source's illusion—illusion with a capital "I"—where everything is experienced in shorthand. Here, life is mostly about saying the right words, doing the right things, thinking appropriate thoughts, and feeling appropriate feelings. Consider politics, movies, church, industry, romance, and social life. Here, life is all about appearance and measuring up, *including how you appear to yourself and measure up to your own standards.*

The second level is more about noticing when words and actions don't match and noticing when then they do. This can be delightfully revealing when you begin to discover that your words and actions, thoughts and feelings, aren't congruent. You think one thing and say another. Of course, most of us substitute guilt and shame for delight. Then it's off to therapy or alcohol or drugs or withdrawal and so on. But it doesn't have to be that way.

On the next level, you can observe what anyone or anything demonstrates, including yourself, without judgment. This is called noticing. Now you begin to trust the support that these three dimensions provide. Now no one can fool you for long with words or doing, *including you.* That's right, you can no longer fool yourself with your *own* words and actions, thoughts and feelings. This is the beginning of real freedom. Here, the most interesting realities show up—hearing what can't quite be "heard," seeing what can't quite be "seen," feeling what can't be "felt." Spiritual dimensions will naturally present themselves without the traumas usually associated with spiritual awakening.

Remember I said earlier that unless love is expressed from these three dimensions, it is usually just a good idea? The expression I'm describing is another name for demonstrating. I'm not talking about getting out in the "real world" and "doing good works" rather than just thinking about it. The latter is often just more doing, where everything is still perceived in shorthand. When someone demonstrates these three dimensions, when someone expresses love *from* these three dimensions, everything they do is a "good work."

What is the final level of noticing? What all of the above rests in—the context. This is the fundamental mystery, and words and concepts (as well as feelings) will only get in your way of experiencing this. Don't struggle for the words and concepts to experience it; simply experience everything all at once. This is the simplest event possible; all the rest of it is complicated.

Overweight horse hockey

Q. Can you trust what someone does? Can you trust their "doing"?

Now that is a really interesting question and points to differences between doing and demonstrating.

Let's ask an earlier question. "How tall am I?"

You may respond that I am about six feet tall. You could verify that with a tape measure, but look again. Without any tape measure, check it out: how tall am I?

I'm suggesting that you don't need a tape measure or anything else to compare and contrast my height with, to notice that I am "just this tall." Now this is *not* a play on words, logical tautology, or truism. If I sat down, how tall would I be? Now the words may be the same, in that I am also "just this tall," but no one would be confused by the direct perception of how tall I am in different circumstances. Get it? You can directly perceive or notice how tall I am, without any other aids. I'm not suggesting you'll notice I am five feet, eleven and one-half inches tall; rather, you'll directly notice that my head is "just this far" from my feet and "just this far" from the ceiling. No inches or centimeters are involved here. Once you learn to recognize with noticing, you will be astounded by what can be directly perceived by your awareness.

Be patient, sweethearts; I am answering your question. What can be directly noticed *is* what is being demonstrated, and this includes much, much more than "sensory awareness." In fact, it includes everything all at once.

For example, you can always notice the momentary play of emotions across someone's face. In fact, you can try observing this when you are in a place that allows some quiet observation that will not disturb those around you. When done successfully, it may seem as if the face is actually morphing or changing shape right in front of you. This is not a hallucination. Remember earlier when I asked you to notice what color my shirt was? It turned out it wasn't just light tan, but in fact a whole palette of tans and light and shading. Were you imagining all those shades of tan? As soon as your attention is directed, it becomes obvious that those colors really exist out there. The same is true with an individual's facial expressions. There is never just one expression but a whole palette of emotions—even if you don't have the words or concepts to describe or measure what you notice. You can still notice it all. When you begin to notice in this way, they may look like many different versions of themselves, nearly simultaneously. Thus, you can notice emerging or unexpressed feelings, moods, and anticipations. Isn't it amazing? Of course, this panoply of emotions was probably outside of your awareness until now, and the person was almost certainly unaware of all these emotions.

At first, all of this you may or may not actually "see." Your noticing may only be felt as a vague sense of trust or attraction, or mistrust and repulsion.

Noticing is not really a course in training or sharpening your five senses, although this will naturally happen. Noticing is more a course in returning your attention to "what is" rather than what you think or feel about "what is." Almost all of what you normally think and feel about "what is" is some version of "what isn't"—a personal or cultural daydream that separates you from reality and the inherent support that reality is always providing.

So what am I demonstrating? Among many things, I am demonstrating my height or how far the top of my head is from the floor, whether standing, lying, or sitting.

So what am I "doing"? Really very little. I may be standing very still, or talking animatedly, or finger-painting my body with tempera paints, but I will continue to *effortlessly* demonstrate my height, independent of all that other doing. What is being demonstrated is always effortless. *Not* noticing what is being demonstrated is what takes effort. I sometimes say, "Not being enlightened is the hardest work you will ever do."

> *Not being enlightened is the hardest work you'll ever do.*

● ● ●

Now I may tell you that I love you, and go on to, what? Give you a ring, open a joint checking account, adopt your children from a previous marriage, sexually satisfy you, buy you chocolates, be faithful? And then one day, all too soon, I announce that I never really loved you at all and must leave to pursue a career in overweight horse hockey.

Did all or any of that doing prove that I loved you? Can you trust what someone does? If their words and their actions can't be trusted, then what can be trusted?

If you count on trusting someone's doing, you will find yourself saying, "But he said and did all the right things." Now you may suggest that we need to investigate the other party's intentions, expectations, psychological mechanisms, self-deceptions, and definitions of love; all of this can be useful, informative, entertaining, temporarily successful, and all too soon fail miserably where it matters most—in your actual life.

The truth is you can't always trust what someone does, either—all their doing is just what gets done—but you can always trust what they demonstrate. You just have to stay tuned through noticing.

The same applies to you. Others in your life are trying to trust your words and doing. They want to believe that your words are true and that what you do means what they hope it does. But you know it isn't always that easy, right?

How can they trust what you say and do when *you* can't always trust what you say and do? Things change, shift happens, *you change*. So you try to explain to them, "Yes I married you, and took out a mortgage with you, and told you I would love you forever, but it's different now. I'm different, and you're different, so I'm getting out."

Why didn't they notice the changes that were incrementally happening? Why didn't you recognize what was happening? Why was anyone surprised by this development? From where I sit, the reality of a life situation, another human being, or yourself is being fully demonstrated all the time, even if you don't have the words or concepts to describe it. Like that big green avocado, *this is reality showing up whole. This is reality showing up all at once.*

One trait of "reality showing up whole" is that you will never have sufficient words or concepts to describe it. That's just the way it is, and that is very good news. Trust that you can notice how it is. Trust that you will *always* notice how it is, and that returning your attention to how it *is* will dramatically reduce miscommunication, disillusionment, and hurt feelings.

The meaning of the words is the easiest part to get. Don't focus on the meaning of the words *or* actions; just keep noticing in three dimensions. When I look out at you, I cannot see you apart from the wall behind you, the floor under you, the ceiling above you. I cannot hear your voice apart from the telephone ringing in the other room, the people breathing, the sound of the fan. This is the context we're all in today. In noticing what's actually here to be seen, heard, and felt, what I feel about you I cannot feel apart from the sensation of the air on my skin, the weight resting on the soles of my feet, the itch on the back of my neck. From this place, there is nothing that can't be noticed. This is what it means to tune in—to return your attention to what can be directly noticed in three dimensions.

Q. So how do you tell what they are demonstrating if you can't tell by their doing?

I appreciate and empathize with the frustration in your question. I agree that if someone says the right things, and their doing supports what they say, then what else can you do? If someone is a naturally great con person—and you all are—are you powerless to protect yourself?

One common element in every con, including self-cons, is the desire of the participants to have what is said and done be true. In general, when someone or some life situation supports what you want to be true about the world around you, and most importantly, what you want to be true about yourself, you experience rapport and some positive or at least neutral feeling toward the person or situation.

On the other hand, if an individual or life situation does not support what you want to be true, almost everyone feels the loss of rapport and may become angry, blaming, and quite critical. In these situations, an opportunity is either gained or lost. I recommend that you use this opportunity to acknowledge but not believe, at least not believe completely, any feelings of anger, hatred, blame, or jealousy. Keep returning to noticing the other person or situation. Behind the appearance of fragmentation, separation, and loss is a fundamental wholeness that cannot be tarnished.

Temporarily suspend your desire for what someone says to be true. Temporarily suspend the meaning that you attach to what they do. Isn't that how actions become "true"? Don't you say quietly to yourself or out loud, "This (action) means that he loves me," or "This means that he doesn't love me"? Temporarily let go of the meaning.

Another way to say this is, if you have a strong preference for what they say or do to be true, you stop noticing the whole of the person or situation—*you stop noticing what else is true.* Why would anyone do this? Because the "rest of what's true" probably doesn't support what *you want* to be true. The more selective you are in what you want to be true, the less you notice *and the less you allow reality to support you.*

Coming home

So the more you are able to give up your preferences for what you want to be true, or what you want to have happen, the more you support reality and the more reality can support you.

How is it that reality can support you when you support reality? What can a statement like this possibly mean? Briefly, here's a review of how noticing gets you there.

Begin by *noticing* the three dimensionality of everything surrounding you wherever you are, and *accept* what you notice just as it is, including your three-dimensional self. This means acceptance without preferring anything to be different. If you do this, you will automatically experience a simple yet exquisite *appreciation* for all this stuff just as it is. Why? Because what you are noticing and accepting, in a very ordinary way, *is* what is real. When you perceive in this way, you begin to notice and support the inherent wholeness that surrounds you. The really good news is that this wholeness always includes you. This is what I call supporting reality.

From this place, you always get to discover what, if anything, there is for you to do about "it," whether "it" is another human being, a life situation, or yourself. Whatever this "doing" is, it will always have you behaving with natural *competence*. Your life gets much, much, easier. You become happier. You behave with fewer false starts, missteps, and detours.

Typically, you will discover that there is much less for you to do than you think. This is natural competence.

So what is it to notice the whole of a person or life situation? When you notice someone, begin with these three dimensions. Notice their height, width, colors, textures, the sounds in the room, how far their head is from the ceiling, the empty spaces between them and the other objects in the room, space and silence between sounds, and remember to include the physical sensations that you feel.

All of this stuff is the context in which life situations and actual human beings exist. You can only understand something in its context. The more broad or vast the context is that you can observe, without leaving *your* immediate context, the more profound and spontaneous your understanding. So stay in your immediate context—keep returning your attention to your present surroundings. Let's call this returning to our common context.

All this stuff, including you, exists first and most importantly in three dimensions. What you normally think and feel *about* all this stuff exists only in two dimensions. So when you notice, begin by suspending what you normally think and feel. Noticing is not just more thinking or feeling. Does this sound simplistic? I hope so. Living the liberated life is so simple—really. It is just too obvious.

This is what the present always offers, without exception: you get to come *home*, finally home, right where you have always been, when not confused by what you normally feel and think. Your recognition of home will be unmistakable, undeniable, and ultimately irrevocable. "I'm home." This is the power of *here*—this is the power of noticing. All the stuff around you, including your body, is a tremendous help in experiencing *here*.

Your spiritual journey will be so much easier, so much more efficient, when you journey without leaving home, without abandoning yourself, scattering your only family, and denying your true friends. Coming home is the end of the trials of separation.

Chapter 8
Some Advice

Sometimes students have an area or two that trip them up regularly. These selections of conversations offer advice in specific areas. As dialogues, they demonstrate what is said and lead the listener to more resourceful states.

Acceptance

Q. How do I accept what is, as it is? This is the hardest part for me.

When what you notice aligns with how things actually are, you support the universe and allow the universe, in turn, to support you. Noticing means to notice what actually is. Noticing begins with the senses. What do you see? What do you hear? You can begin by noticing your physical surroundings. Take a moment now and follow these instructions.

Look around you—see the things around you. Notice their color; notice that objects are not just one color—that light and shadow and texture create shades of color. Notice which objects are closer to you and which are farther away. Notice their different elevations relative to you. Are they above you or below you? Are they to the left or to the right? Notice what might be moving or vibrating.

Now find something in the room that you are neutral about. Something that you have no strong preference for or against. Got one? Good. Now just like an actor might do, prefer that it be closer to you. Strongly pretend that it needs to be closer to you. Let it disturb you that it's just that far away. Imagine your life being so much better if it were closer to you. How does that feel? A strong preference to have something, anything—a person, a place, a situation—be different from it is, is always a kind of disturbance. Welcome to the world of preferences.

Would it surprise you to know that preferences are a kind of "overlay" or filter that censors what you perceive? These filters work by distorting and deleting what is perceived. The good news is that you can learn to accept what is perceived out there in the world—including yourself, without preference. This is called noticing.

Because noticing always precedes your thinking, noticing "what is" always precedes your desire to have "what is" be different. This is a natural ability that cannot be taken from you.

Begin acceptance of "what is" by recognizing that you have preferences. Acknowledge that your preferences are all about your thinking and feeling and not really about the world out there.

Q. But that is how I motivate myself, and get things done. I want things to be different than they are. Isn't this how we make the world a better place?

You are absolutely right. Americans historically have done as much as anyone to change the world—to alter what is. Our humanitarian efforts should be remembered in future history as legendary. We're responsible for more inventions, innovations, and relief of real and apparent suffering than anyone else.

Did you know, however, that most of our national doing, our continuous activity to solve real and imagined problems, is itself the result of previous doing? The same is true for almost everyone I meet and talk with. They want to know in their own lives what to do, how to fix or repair something that is *itself* the result of previous doing. Am I suggesting that you do nothing? No. I am suggesting that you only do what needs doing, which is almost always a lot less than what you imagine you need to do.

Someone says to me that they want to take control over some part of their life. I might ask them, "Have you accepted whatever this is, just as it is?" Usually they'll reply, "Of course not. That's why I want to change it. If I accepted it, then wouldn't that mean that that's the way I want it to be? Wouldn't I be condoning and approving of people and situations that are wrong?"

Right and wrong is a kind of illusion. In some ways, it is the most pervasive of preferences or filters. Our inability to see "what is", including ourselves, others, and our life situation, without the lens of right and wrong, good and bad, blinds all of us. Humanity is most incompetent when believing itself wronged and therefore right—right and justified in creating even more pain and misery.

Seeking to change something because it is *wrong,* without first accepting it just as it is, almost always guarantees that you will create more problems, but noticing always leads to competence in every situation. How does that happen? By accepting everything that you notice, which means noticing without preference.

For as long as it lasts, look around you and let everything you see be in exactly the right place. Let everything around you be at exactly the right elevation, exactly the right colors. Now drop the word "right." Just let everything be where it is and how it is. That is the acceptance that I'm talking about. You accept things neither as right nor wrong, but as they are. Soon you will begin to taste the exquisite peace that comes from accepting in this way. As you look around you, what *in and of itself* needs changing—what needs changing outside of your preferences? You will discover that very little "needs" changing.

Q. Dropping the word "right" sounds like a way to justify whatever someone wants to do.

It does, doesn't it? Before enlightenment, while people are still struggling in the middle, this sounds like a convenient escape. With an experience of the end and the perfection inherent in all things, everything shifts. With moments of noticing, you will sense and appreciate the shift.

Living in a world of right and wrong is a kind of illusion. And there is nothing wrong with anyone's illusion—when all is going well. When all is not going well, you suffer. Why suffer more than you do? Reality (and enlightenment) are outside of right and wrong, but it is *not* what you make up. It is *not* a subjective experience. It is about "what is," exactly as it is. Reality is always being demonstrated. More importantly, it can be noticed here and now—always in the here and now.

The more you practice accepting everything outside of right or wrong, the easier it becomes to behave competently. You will naturally do what it is that needs doing. Now drop the word "need," and you discover that you are doing whatever it is you are doing. See how easy life can be?

Have you ever noticed how much easier it sometimes is to like someone else's life, or be comfortable in someone else's house? Everyone hopefully has fewer preferences about their neighbors' dust bunnies or unwashed dishes.

Often when men and women and boys and girls are falling in love with each other, they are able to accept so much about the other person. She may even say, "Well, it's not that I like or dislike the shirt tail that keeps creeping out of his pants. That's just how he is." Hopefully in those relationships a good long time passes before you decide that the other person must change. Because when you do decide, most likely you will have stopped accepting the other person. Then I pretty much guarantee that you will not behave competently with them. You will stand the process on its head. You will begin with wanting to control them. You will substitute control for competence.

Q. Aren't there some circumstances that need changing in everyone's life or in the world?

I have noticed that things do change and they seem to change whether they needed to or not. I don't think "need" has much to do with it.

Imagine your child has spilled grape juice in the middle of your living room floor. Just notice that the stain *itself* doesn't need cleaning or not cleaning. Now you might prefer to clean it up, but from the perspective of enlightenment, the stain itself is done. The whole world is already done. It exists outside of your preferences.

You may need your children to be different from who they are, but try noticing your children with acceptance—perhaps initially when they don't see you looking at them in this way. Now accept them just as they are, right then, right there, beginning with what you see and hear. Everyone I've ever watched practice this demonstrates the most delightful appreciation for their child, along with perhaps a few tears or small gasps, just as if they are rediscovering a precious gift they had misplaced.

Do you know what your children will notice if they catch you noticing and accepting them in this way? Pure appreciation for them exactly as they are. This is what you saw in your child's face for at least the first year of life. Especially as a small baby, when he or she looked at you and everything around them, just noticing, just accepting. Were they demonstrating competence? Absolutely. Think of everything they learned. Were they living in perfection? Absolutely. Parents sometimes tell me as their children grow that what they miss most of those early months is being beheld in their child's eyes.

Noticing your child or loved one in this way is what I call "unconditioned attention"— attention without preference for what is noticed. From my perspective, God gives us unconditioned attention nonstop. There is no time during the day or night in our lives that we don't have God's attention. God's attention is the force that breathes existence into everything, animate and inanimate. God notices and accepts you exactly as you are.

How do you practice acceptance? Begin practicing acceptance of the little stuff, the things that you're relatively neutral about. Sit noticing the socks on the floor and the rest of the room from that place of acceptance. Imagine that your husband or your child walks in full of their preferences and expectations of you, and you accept all they are, too. Appreciating them in all their complexity, you discover what, if anything, you actually need to do with their preferences and expectations of you. When you practice this acceptance often enough and long enough, you may well discover that your natural competence has you doing other activities or responding to situations in ways that may be much different from what you do now. You may even become a spiritual teacher. How? By simply demonstrating to your husband and children the power of noticing and the natural competence that follows both for you and them.

I have seen again and again that when I notice my students and accept them just as they are, they experience what they describe as an almost unbearable appreciation for themselves, and they demonstrate increasing competence in all areas of their lives.

Q. I've practiced what you talk about. I sat in a quiet place in my home and noticed my grandmother's throw rug and how it is starting to fray. When I notice it as you describe,

I find myself thinking about my grandmother, her life, her passing, and all that represents to me, including the times when she was not especially nice to me. A lot of who I am today comes from my grandmother. I would like the rug to stay in better condition, but I don't want to just store it in the closet. So I guess this is just the way it is. The fraying carpet is really a perfect representation of all of that. Then I happened to think about my ex-husband, and for many moments I accepted him just the same way. I felt free and wonderful, and then the feeling passed. He's just too close in my life. We share our children, but his support payments are often late. He knows how to push my buttons. It's easy for me to be angry and upset with him, but I now know that it's possible to accept him in the way that you talk about because I did it. But it seems no matter how hard I try, I can't accept him the rest of the time.

Congratulations on noticing so much about your experience and acknowledging to yourself when you don't meet your own expectations. Just say it out loud: "I can't accept him most of the time." Why would you want to acknowledge this out loud? Because that's "what is." The harder you try to change the way things are without first accepting them, including your own feelings, the less progress you may make. So stop trying. *Accept that you can't accept him* and that's just the way it is for now and maybe for some time into the future. This is accepting what can't be accepted.

Another woman I know was having a similar problem. She was in an open relationship with a man, and it mostly worked for both of them. But there were some aspects of his behavior that she was sure were wrong. She just couldn't accept that he desired other women. It would come through in cycles and temporarily drive her crazy with jealousy. Trying to change him didn't work, and trying to change her thinking also didn't work because she was sure that she was right. She still continued to notice what wasn't working. No matter how much she noticed, she still couldn't accept the way things were. Finally, she gave up the fight with herself and just *noticed* that she couldn't accept things the way they were and *accepted* that she couldn't accept them. She immediately felt peaceful. In this way, she got the results she wanted. She thought that it was sort of like a card trick or sleight of hand, but it worked! She got peaceful and noticed that her thinking—and feelings—began to change all by themselves.

The same held true for things she couldn't accept about herself—that she really was a jealous person. When she accepted this, her behaviors became more thoughtful and more generous all by themselves. She had reached natural competence. Almost magically, her husband's behavior also changed, and together they came into balance with each other.

Going deep, getting light

Q. How do I let go of an upset?

By noticing the effect your thinking has on you. Yesterday we got a call from a student who was upset with his life situation. He said that he was debating with his wife, who is also a student, the value of living a genuinely spiritual life—that is, of really noticing "what is," exactly as it is. In this case, "what is" is their relationship. Their problems are plain to both of them, but he refuses to accept what they both clearly notice.

This is a tough spot—to successfully notice how things are and then try to debate yourself and someone you love out of the noticing. This is crazy making and he knew it, but he was resourceful enough to talk about it with us right in the middle of his anger. I suggested that he make a genuine inquiry. I asked him, "How is the debate working for you?" He paused for a long time. His upset three hundred miles away was palpable in our kitchen. Could he notice the effect of his own thinking on himself in the moment? When he does, when he grasps the cost of having his attention on "what isn't" in the presence of "what is," his suffering ends—every time. He finally acknowledged to himself that arguing for his illusions really wasn't working, and that opened the door for competency to show up.

So how are your debates working for you? Let me suggest a simple guideline: *what is more true for you, rather than less true for you, has you feel lighter.* The process of awakening for almost everyone that I meet involves going deep and getting light. Can you get light without going deep? *Yes!* Is it as rare as hen's teeth? Also, yes. So just expect that you'll go deep a bunch. In the process, you'll probably get stuck a bunch, too, so it's best not to believe any of those "deep" thoughts. How can you recognize a "deep" thought? You will feel more separate and fragmented, less whole rather than more whole.

> *What is more true for you, rather than less true for you, has you feel lighter.*

When discovering what is true for you, follow the thread of lightness. When you're not enjoying the illusion, you have certainly gone deep. The more intense the feelings of anger, sadness, jealousy, or despair, the more illusion and reality are overlapping. This is an opportunity. This is a chance to have all of your noticing practice show up.

As you begin to notice the effect of your thinking and feeling on yourself and those around you, you may have a responsibility to lighten up. Ask yourself: what do I feel when I think this thought? Do I feel heavier or lighter? Keep following the lightness. *What is more true for you, rather than less true, will feel lighter and lighter until you reach enlightenment.* Remember, it's not called "enheavyment."

Along the way, you may become temporarily sarcastic, or biting, or cynical *and* feel somewhat lighter. Congratulations. Notice the caustic element of your feeling and thinking, and keep inquiring. What is most true for you will not be corrosive. It will be whole and expansive. You will feel whole and expansive when you think it. It will include the object of your thought and the rich context that it rests in, *including you*. That's right, the "including you" is your part to play in all of "it"—whatever it is. Your part will always feel simple or at ease or light no matter how complex the situation may seem at other times. Trust that feeling of lightness. Trust the simple perfection apart from your preferences.

The dark night of the soul

Q. How do I deal with loss and grief?

During this life, we will all lose everything that we value—everything that we love. This includes the toys and friends of our early childhood, as well as our careers, companions, possessions, and loved ones. None of this will go with us during the passage we call death, or so it seems.

How do we cope with this loss and resulting grief? With all the wisdom and skill you possess. What else can you do? If the loss is great, then the grief may well be deep and long. This is not the time for false bravado and intellectual understanding alone.

During your grief, there will be times when the suffering will abate—your mind will calm and your heart is more at ease. Notice these moments and let them prevail for however long they last. Do not go looking for the source of your pain. The storm will ebb and flow and eventually it will pass. It always does, doesn't it?

The path of spiritual maturity includes going deep and getting light. In the depths of your pain, you may choose not to believe any of the thoughts that show up. These include the "what if," "if only," and "why me" thoughts, just to name a few. You may choose to notice how you feel during the periods of calm and at ease, and the thoughts that show up then—although don't be surprised if there are very few thoughts, just a sense of settled acceptance.

> *Remember, it's not called "enheavyment."*

If you are not now experiencing this terrible grief, use the "little deaths"—the small everyday losses—to practice the art of noticing. I have observed that we always get what we practice, and we are always practicing something.

Q. What about the heavy emotions? How do we deal with them long-term, such as a mid-life crisis?

There are many ways to achieve profound noticing, including through intense suffering—pain, loss, death, and separation. So there is nothing wrong with the heavy emotions.

From time to time I work with people who are dying, or have just discovered that their child has a life-threatening illness, or their primary relationship has ended. In each case, their suffering would seem to be insurmountable. They may have lost the ability to sleep or relax or find any comfort in life. It is not too much to say that the experience of grief or loss is living *through* them. They are not having the experience; it is having them. And in the midst of this intense and numbing emotional suffering, they want to know what to do. If the suffering is deep enough and long enough, nothing they try will work for very long.

They will say to me, "Nothing I try is working. What I used to do simply isn't working." And they are right. But the problem is not in them or in their abilities. They are not suffering to appease an angry god or right imagined sins.

You may ask of Source, "How can I lessen the pain?" or "What do I do?" and receive a meaningful answer. By all means, employ it. Learn to receive and use reliable guidance from Source in the ways I've already described.

But don't be surprised if these messages are infrequent and do not produce the immediate results you want. You may not be doing anything wrong. Source certainly isn't doing anything wrong. Put your noticing practice to work as best you can. Accept, on faith if necessary, that something important is unfolding.

You may be experiencing a significant mid-life passage or something much more profound, the dark night of the soul. Both of these may be accompanied by what surely seems to be an enormous life reversal—the loss of a career, or loved one, or your health. In either case, everything that you have based your life on progressively loses its meaning.

The most significant difference between the mid-life passage and the dark night of the soul is how long they last, and this is a big difference. With duration, the effects of disillusionment and loss of meaning are compounded both in the world out there—that is, in your living an effective life in culture—*and* inside you, where your soul may struggle to find comfort.

When all of your familiar strategies "out there" don't work, such as watching TV or reading or talking with friends, you would hope to find comfort inside, yet this is the epicenter of what isn't working, or so it seems. When one's most intimately held beliefs—your religion, your traditions, or more simply the essence of who you thought you were—no longer serve or protect, then what?

The fundamental experience of these times is *the loss of control.*

In our lives, we have all had times when we could not control our emotions—a sudden infatuation or envy of a friend's success when our own struggle seems unrewarded. Powerful emotions have swept through all of us, and then they are gone. But a mid-life passage may last for many months or years. The dark night of the soul is often described as lasting an average of seven years. My own lasted longer than that—and I apologize for even suggesting that I might know how long your life passage may last. Each experience is unique.

Yet the experience of increasing loss of control during a dark night of the soul is universal. I have been reminded that surely this dark night of the soul must be just another grand illusion created by the mind. Viewed from the outside, this is true; but when experienced from the inside, the inner turmoil—the perpetual existential nightmares, the increasing lack of sleep and endless self-doubts, the inability to communicate the depth and intensity of this raw falling to pieces—coupled with a deteriorating ability to look and act "normal," becomes hands-down the most real experience you have ever had.

We always get what we practice, and we are always practicing something.

You may know intellectually that this is all an illusion and will pass, but as the very cells in your body threaten dissolution, you realize that to deny the reality of what is happening is to risk death.

So you must begin, step by step, to embrace what you thought could not be embraced, to endure what cannot be endured, to dance with the most unwanted of partners. And in the depth of uninterrupted night, your soul—unmoored and unguided—must find a way.

This is the soul's work, and it is a messy affair. This is the essence of being Only Human, and apparently no one is immune. A great teacher with whom I studied for several years has entered the dark night of the soul. It is now living through him. He has lost sixty pounds, and looks the better for it. His arrogance and audacity have been stripped from him. His sudden bursts of crying and grief are as unbidden and genuine as his former yogic feats. The phenomenal control he was gifted with is gone—so gone, it is as if he never had it. It would seem that he is being boiled down to his heart essence, and his mind, his incredible clarity of mind, wasn't invited along.

So what is the point of this dark night of the soul? If there were only one way to describe the outcome of all this suffering, I would say it is *a great softening of the individual.* My observation is that the dark night of the soul is toughest on those of us who needed to be in control the most. Sometimes the need for control came from chaotic childhoods; sometimes there was no obvious cause, yet all who have suffered the most were least able to surrender control.

My former teacher describes his day and night experience as "hard" and "edgy" and exhausting. My own included experiencing weeks of feeling like I was encased in solid granite. It was as if the very air around my body was so dense that I could not breathe or move with any ease. *Everything* seemed so hard.

I remember when I finally began to soften into the experience. Every morning I felt overwhelmed after another night of lucid dreams, where I was confronted again and again with all that needed healing in my life. Again, archetypal beings had appeared in the night to help—not the angels I hoped for, but powerful dispassionate beings who had little patience for my bumbling and lack of understanding. I could not remember the last time I had anything approaching a normal night's sleep, but there I was, out of bed and faced with another day of being a husband and father and employer with employees and customers and all that that demanded. Mine was a life built on control and accomplishment, a life that required *someone* to be in charge.

But that morning I said "fuck it" and laughed—something I hadn't done much of in years. I thought, "If it takes me three tries and four times as long to do some ordinary task, then so be it. If I don't act or appear normal, then so be it. This is just the way it is." And a wonderful thing happened. For a whole day I breathed and relaxed and surrendered control. This was not giving up; this was giving in. By softening into the experience, I stopped resisting the awful mystery and started dancing with it.

Why "awful" mystery? Because that is how it felt. My thinking and plans for the future, my need to preserve propriety, my need to act and appear normal could not compete with what was happening to me, and it was simply awe-full. For almost twelve months, my physical body was in pain for no apparent reason. Medical doctors could find no cause. All of this was an enormous mystery to me. My plans for the future and the present simply did not include a spiritual awakening. Here I was being remade without my permission, and with no concern for my comfort or convenience.

Why dancing? As I learned more about this process of awakening, I stopped asking, "Why me?" and instead began to ask, "How can I help?" When I stopped trying to lead and began to follow, the process was less painful, and my life became easier. I learned that I had to follow with intelligence and discernment. I had to stay tuned because the dance steps would change. At times I was expected to lead!

Sometimes this dancing was a waltz, at other times a dance of primitive abandon, but at all times I had to pay attention to what I felt. I had to listen to my heart. I had to let go of control and soften into my emotions. Being edgy and hard with myself and hardhearted with others just did not work.

You don't have to own your own business or have any children or fit into any special group to begin an awakening. In fact, who gets nominated and who doesn't really is a mystery. In many ways, we are all dedicated to control in our lives. The important question is, "When control isn't working, do you notice?" If you do, you will begin to return to your natural competence. If you don't notice, then Source will continue to massage your resistance until you do. Either way, it's progress.

Part IV
Living a Genuinely
Spiritual Life

Introduction

The fruit of the beginning is living a genuinely spiritual life, which has almost nothing and sometimes everything to do with religion. After practicing noticing, you will discover your will becoming aligned with God's will—the basis of genuine prayer—and you will demonstrate your own natural awakening with ever-growing competence. A genuinely spiritual life could be described as fluid, flexible, and intelligent.

Remember earlier I said that when you are not living in the present, beliefs and principles are what sustain you? They are a meager but necessary ration on your journey to discovering Avocado Consciousness—the wholeness of everything all at once. For this journey, you cannot pack or store or accumulate the present because it cannot be preserved. There is no way to dry it or freeze it or can it. What can be preserved? What are ideal for freezing and drying and canning? Beliefs and principles. During our natural confusion and heartache and despair, haven't we all chewed and gnawed on our principles and beliefs to see us through? Haven't we all choked and experienced firsthand how stale these rations are and pleaded for something greater than ourselves to restore the freshness of life to us?

When this freshness and fluidity arrives, there is no mistaking it for our meager rations. In the present, the internal debates end. All of our suffering finds its own natural context to rest in. Perspective is vast and all is revealed with no need to know anything in particular. This is noticing. This is embracing that pause that precedes all of your thinking and judging.

Can this happen within religions? Can Christians and Muslims and Jews and others discover themselves in the present? Absolutely. I see it all the time. From the present, the original juiciness of Christ's message and Buddha's teachings is effortlessly revealed—not as the way, but simply pointing the way. But the bureaucracy of religion does not trust the present, does not trust the stirring that noticing eventually brings. There is precious little room for new prophets.

Living a genuinely spiritual life may well include the bureaucracy of beliefs and principles from time to time. If it does, make the best use of them that you can. But don't confuse the destination with the compass.

Chapter 9
The Power of Prayer

Regular prayer or meditation is often considered a part of living a genuinely spiritual life. But what is prayer? How do you pray? How do you know if your prayers are successful? Does it have anything to do with getting what you want?

Students and visitors often ask me about prayer. Prayer is not something I normally talk about, but the truth is I do pray—all the time. How I pray may sound unusual compared to most ideas of prayer. But from my perspective, what I do and how I do it gets to the very heart of how to pray successfully—what I call the "power of prayer."

Start by getting quiet or still, clearing your mind a little. You may want to turn off the television and unplug the phone to help you be in a respectful way, a way of humility to communicate with Source. Part of the reason we get into a respectful, humble space with God is to become something like God. Surely Source is not hurried or distracted, and neither should we be if we want to pray successfully. Being in a still, quiet place, clearing your mind a little, and letting the day's worries go is a good way to begin. Most importantly, *pause* before you go on and request what it is you want of God.

It is in this pause that you will discover the power of prayer.

Be like God

Some people believe that if they are in favor with God, then God will give them what they want. You could be asking for something for yourself, like a new car, or you could be asking for your child or loved one to heal. The power of prayer is about increasing your chances that you're going to get what is wanted. The question is, what do you really want?

Now I'm going to suggest something important. As you pause in that moment before prayer, for just a little while, *be like God.*

The chief difference that I perceive between God and most everyone else is this: God always votes for what is going to happen next, while most individuals vote for having it their way. And right up front I'll suggest a radical principle—that when you get exactly what you want through prayer, *you get what was going to happen next.*

And that's exactly what it means to *be like God*, to have God's favor, to be in the flow, to be in communion with God, to receive God's grace. Remember, all around us is God's creation. This physical world, this world that we live in, is the best, most obvious demonstration of God. God wants "what is," exactly as it is, including you. And my proof of that is that *this is* what's here.

We can all get into trouble by putting our attention on what isn't here, especially when we begin to pray. In the presence of "what is," we go to God and say, "You know, my life looks pretty good, but frankly, I want to fine tune it a bit. Maybe I want to fine tune it a lot, because I don't think it's the way it should

God always votes for what is going to happen next.

be." If that request to have it be different comes from a place of not respecting and appreciating how in fact it is, your chances of getting what it is you want are slim. It isn't going to happen. Consider this—if what you want and what God wants are two different things, who's probably going to win? Whom would you bet on? God, right?

As a humble human being, it would be nice to have Source on your side. What I want to suggest is that Source is always on your side. But what is it that you want?

Back to that wanting, back to that prayer, back to that asking for something to be different from how it is. Most people have a number of things to pray for—to heal someone who is sick, to get through a tough time, to have their lives work better.

But hopefully in your life, in your practice of prayer, perhaps in that pause before asking for what you want, you will have that incredible experience of surrendering your will to God's will. "Not my will, God, but yours."

Consider that all around you, every day, is the most amazing demonstration of God's will. Wherever you are right now, check it out. Everything you see and hear, everything you might physically bump up against is God's creation, including your life and everyone else's. This is at this time, in this way, how God wants it to be. So for five minutes a day—even thirty seconds a day—*want exactly what it is you already have.*

There is incredible power in wanting your life to be exactly as it is, even if it is only a sixty-second pause before you pray.

Try this simple exercise now. Wherever you are, want some object in your office or home or car to be exactly where it is. It could be a potted plant hanging from the ceiling, a pen sitting on the table, or an air freshener in your car. Try wanting it to be in the exact location it is.

Then, just for a moment, after you've got that clearly in your mind and heart, try wanting it to be a different color. Now really want it to be that way. Have it be so that your life will not be successful and you will not find peace unless the green air freshener is blue or the yellow daisy is red. How do you feel when you do that?

I know this sounds like a silly example, but consider it when you are asking God to change things from the way they are to the way you want them to be.

What do you want?

The power of prayer begins with noticing how things are, and accepting them exactly as they are, without preferences for them to be otherwise. And if you do this successfully, you will find yourself appreciating things exactly as they are. This is what it means to love. This is what it means to be God's eyes and ears—to see and hear everything just as it is.

Then, from that place of appreciation for the way things actually are, check it out. Of all your wants, which ones start to fall away? You'll notice that from that place of absolutely loving everything exactly as it is, your will comes into line with God's will.

I'm not saying this doesn't take time and practice—it does. But when it does happen, it happens very quickly. You'll bring your plan in line with the universe's plan and life becomes easy—incredibly easy.

You know those moments of flow you experience? Those moments when everything seems to click? Sometimes it's not when you win the raffle or you get proposed to or your UPS package shows up on time. Often, it's just in the middle of the most ordinary events, the most mundane day. One day just walking through the park watching your children play, something falls into place. You're being moved in the universe just like everything else is being moved, and you feel an incredible sense of well-being.

When you want your life to be exactly like it is and your will coincides with God's, you develop a natural competency toward what it is you will pray for, for what it is you want next.

That darn dam

The point of prayer really isn't to ask for what you want, but to surrender your will to God's will. How do you do this? Consider that you're always somewhere, so you're always surrounded by examples of God's will. I'm talking about the chair, the dining room table, your left little fingernail—there they all are. Each physical object has its own integrity and supports you absolutely to the best of its ability. Those chairs and couches will be there for you day or night if you need to sit down. Until the wood starts to crumble and the joints fall apart, they will serve you. Every morning when you get up, the floor you stand on serves you. Every morning when you get up and go outside, the sky is still there.

We live in a most incredibly reliable universe. It's enormously reliable. You wake up in the morning and the dam generating your hydropower and holding back the floodwaters is still standing—day after day, year after year. But let it break, and people will call for an investigation. They'll want to find out who's at fault, who's to blame, why it happened.

What if people occupied their time each day, as an exercise just for fun, investigating why that darn dam is still standing? Or why the sidewalks are still there in the morning? Wouldn't that be amazing?

> *We live in a most incredibly reliable universe.*

Mostly, our attention gets piqued when things don't go the way we want them to. And sometimes the most terrible things do happen. From time to time I work with people who are dying. In the process of preparing for death, there is a stripping away of their most trivial wants, the most trifling changes they once thought were important in their personal lives. Often what remains are just one or two things that are very clear to them, and to me, that it's time to do before they die. In almost every instance, this doing gets done.

Now, did they make it happen? Were they in control? We could make a case that they made it happen. But from my perspective, what happened was that they got slightly ahead of the curve. Getting "ahead of the curve" means they appreciated things exactly as they are just enough that they got to see what was coming next—they got to *want* what was coming next.

What if what you wanted *was* what was coming next? Your wanting would always be satisfied, wouldn't it?

Taking the "Y" out of prayer

Sometimes what makes it difficult about this world that we live in is that we look around at God's handiwork, God's plan, and we throw our hands up and say, "Why? Why? Why are things the way they are? If God were kind and just or even existed, wouldn't they be different?"

A long time ago, I passed up the opportunity to doubt one more time whether God exists. It's clear to me that Source does exist. It shows up in my life all the time that way. Do I have a "handle" on the fundamental mystery? No. Do I regularly get way ahead of the curve? All the time.

So my chief occupation in life is to just love everyone and everything exactly as it is. And from that place of noticing "what is," accepting "what is," and naturally appreciating "what is," natural competence shows up, and you will want what God wants. Can we imagine a more competent being than God? I don't think so. When your will aligns with God's will, you will have natural competence, too.

Remember, the chief difference between human beings and God is that God wants what's going to happen next. God's always satisfied because the world is always exactly the way God wants it. You can find this satisfaction in your own life, too.

So for a little while, be like God. To do this, begin every time with noticing what you sense—notice what you see, what you hear, what you smell. Notice for just five minutes a day, or even just one minute a day. Want the most ordinary things to be exactly as they are.

To love God, love the present

From time to time people ask me, "Is wanting things to be the way they are like being grateful for the good things in my life?"

I make this distinction—that gratitude is a little bit smaller than appreciation. With gratitude, you're grateful for something specific. You may even be grateful that you had a flat tire on the freeway! You didn't make your plane and so you weren't on it when it crashed. What I'm suggesting is to be grateful for everything in your life. That's appreciation.

From my perspective, appreciation is appreciation for "what is," as it is, outside of your preferences, outside of how you would like things to be. Is there anything wrong with how you'd like things to be? No. Would it surprise you to know that God doesn't actually live in a world of right and wrong? That's part of the problem of looking around and judging everything in your life. It all comes out right or wrong, good or bad.

Now I admit, this would all be easier for you if you began this process from living in a state of perfection—if you began this process from your natural enlightenment. Then this kind of appreciation would make a lot more sense to you. And it wouldn't be just intellectual sense; it would be something that you demonstrated regularly in your lives. And people who live genuinely spiritual lives do regularly demonstrate this kind of appreciation.

But don't beat up on yourself if you don't, and don't make learning this difficult for yourself. Begin with noticing simple things that you're neutral about. Begin with your eyes open, with your senses. Pause before praying to get quiet and notice God's creation around you. Let noticing bring you into the present.

Sometimes I say, *if you want to know God, know the present. If you want to love God, love the present.* I also say the same is true of yourself, or your life, or your children. If you want to know your children, be present with them. If you want to love your children, be present with them.

Consider that God loves you unconditionally. What that means is that God does not keep score; there's no tally of rights and wrongs.

You do not qualify or not qualify for God's attention. You get more than one hundred percent of God's attention all the time, no matter what's happening. And you may come to believe this—you may come to know this with your mind. But what I'm talking about is not about beliefs, and it's not about thinking. It's about seeing God's love demonstrated to you everywhere and in every moment. Eventually, you get to demonstrate that love, too. That's demonstrating your natural enlightenment. And with that, living a genuinely spiritual life comes naturally.

Chapter 10
Living a Genuinely Spiritual Life

What is it to live a genuinely spiritual life?

Most people that I talk to who've asked themselves this question assume that they're not. Perhaps they have had experiences of living what they imagine to be a spiritual life, with some success at regular prayer or meditation or fasting or selfless service. Perhaps they have spent significant amounts of time in an ashram or at a meditation center or living with a person or a group that is promising a spiritual life. Yet the contrast between what they think is a spiritual life and the rest of their lives, with its ordinary demands and compromises, leads them to conclude that these moments of spirituality cannot be their whole life. That's why I sometimes say that living a genuinely spiritual life is not what you think.

I have known real monks—folks who meditate ten hours a day, who chant for hours a day, who practice selfless service—and you might be surprised to know that, from time to time, they also wonder if they are living a genuinely spiritual life.

What I've come to learn over the last decade is that living a genuinely spiritual life is not about upgrading your beliefs, your habits, your thoughts, or even your behaviors. Yet there is this popular idea that living a genuinely spiritual life involves certain practices and particularly certain behaviors. But does it? You can chant, meditate hours every day, volunteer your time and service, pray to Jesus Christ, pray to the Hindu gods and goddesses, or emulate Buddha, and none of that is a guarantee that you'll be living a genuinely spiritual life.

I know an enlightened man who's been known to have a drink of wine now and then and to delight in the senses. When questioned about this he said, "Well, consider: in the morning, after you've had something to drink the night before, is it a headache with thoughts of enlightenment, or is it enlightenment with thoughts of a headache?"

Am I advocating indulging your preferences? No. Enlightenment can never be an excuse for simply doing what you want to do. In fact, it has nothing to do with your preferences. It has everything to do with loving the world, including yourself, exactly as it is—and then demonstrating what if anything there is for you to do. This is how you demonstrate your natural enlightenment.

From within enlightenment, you get to understand and have demonstrated to you once and for all that enlightenment is not a state of mind. It's not a state of consciousness. It's not any set of beliefs or behaviors. States of mind come and go; moods come and go. An enlightened person can have a headache in the morning, but what happens to the enlightenment? Nothing! Enlightenment is not a personal matter.

My test for living a genuinely spiritual life is this: *are you demonstrating your natural enlightenment no matter what the circumstances?* That's the punch line. It's the only test. If you are, then you're living a genuinely spiritual life.

So you could well be a monk or that special grandma or granddad that everyone likes to hang out with, who's just there for you and seems wise, or perhaps even just a little bit crazy, a little bit unpredictable in the most delightful or disconcerting ways. They might say very little or talk your ear off. And yet there they are—present, awake, noticing, and loving everything and everyone around them. They're demonstrating their natural enlightenment even as they sit in meditation or on the front porch rocking chair. Living a genuinely spiritual life requires no special circumstances or surroundings.

I get to witness ordinary individuals demonstrating their natural enlightenment fairly often. In those moments, they usually have no context for what enlightenment is, for what it is to live a genuinely spiritual life, so they don't recognize what has happened. In some ways, it's like a pearl that is grasped for a moment and then slips through their fingers. One of my teachers suggested that on my journey, I collect all those enlightened moments like pearls on a string and keep them next to my heart until these moments become my point of reference—until these moments become your point of reference.

Entering the present

Many people experience life as a series of moods. Some of them are up, some of them are down, some of them are boring—just everyday, normal moods. They come, they go, and you are sort of entertained by them. But many moods are not particularly entertaining—or at least before enlightenment they're not. You just wish they'd pass. You wish they'd go away. But what is it that doesn't go away? What is it that persists?

For lack of a better word, I'll call what persists "reality." *Living a genuinely spiritual life is when your perspective coincides with reality.* That's a big statement, isn't it? So the next question is, what is reality? Or as I've been asked before, "Whose reality? In whose opinion?" Good questions, because reality itself doesn't have to do with anyone's opinion. Reality itself persists.

I've also been asked, "Well, is reality like vibrations, perhaps like tiny subatomic particles? Or is reality something like those really tiny moments of now?" I've watched my students in their early process try to escape the past and avoid the future, thinking that the now—the present—is somewhere in that little space that wasn't the past a tenth of a second ago or an hour ago, and is not yet the present five minutes from now. But reality is not some tiny little moment of time or space.

We know that through practices of meditation, of getting still, of quieting the mind, of giving up some of our egoism to selfless service, you can find yourself in the present, in the now, in touch with reality. The same is true through dancing, exercise, art, singing, or sitting on your porch in a rocking chair—one can enter the present.

Living a genuinely spiritual life requires no special circumstances or surroundings.

And when you enter the present and your perspective coincides with reality, with what persists, you effortlessly, organically demonstrate your own natural enlightenment—loving the world, including yourself, exactly as it is, and demonstrating what if anything there is for you to do. In stringing those moments together like pearls, you will live a genuinely spiritual life.

An ordinary, spiritual life

Often the worldly is contrasted with the spiritual, and it can be a useful distinction to make. But those people I know of who are enlightened don't really make a distinction between the worldly and the spiritual, certainly not with students who've been around for a while. Why? Because in moments of enlightenment, you directly perceive that *the worldly is the spiritual* and it isn't somewhere else. It isn't some other time. It's here. It's now.

I've talked with many people who have suggested they would like to pursue a genuinely spiritual life, but first they need to get dinner on the table, get the kids off to school, open a checking account, clean the vacuum cleaner, or wait for retirement. In their minds, they believe they must first do all those things that need doing *before* they can live a genuinely spiritual life.

Moments of enlightenment are never the same experience twice.

Why wait? Why not live a genuinely spiritual life right now? Then go open a checking account, get the kids off to school, and cook a dinner for your husband or lover. That might make quite a difference.

Sometimes people believe they can't live a genuinely spiritual life while their minds are busy with internal chatter. I agree that internal chatter can be a distraction. But I'd like to suggest to you that the internal chatter has a life of its own, and that life need not own you. It's a perfectly organic, evolutionary, natural thing.

I remember the first time I noticed my thinking wasn't in my body but three feet to my left, about head height. I was at peace. And then one day, I discovered that my thinking was gone all together. I couldn't find it, and I didn't miss it. I experienced a tremendously spacious mind—not spaced-out, but spacious.

With thinking out of the way, I could really notice everything around me—and everyone. I got to notice things exactly as they are, accept them as they are, and deeply appreciate them. I deeply fell in love with everyone and everything around me, and I noticed that my competence began to grow. And this experience of living in perfection just keeps growing.

But living a genuinely spiritual life is hard to pin down in practices, and it's hard to pin down in behaviors. No practices or behaviors individually or in any combination are the same as living a genuinely spiritual life. The work of genuine spiritual awakening is not about upgrading your beliefs, and it's not about upgrading the thoughts you have or knowing more. You could even say it's not about becoming a better person. But along the way, interesting things happen. As you begin to demonstrate your natural enlightenment, your beliefs do get upgraded, you do know more about yourself and the world around you, and you become a better person. How can that happen? Because you don't get what you focus on; instead, you get what is beside it. It's like looking at the faint stars at night. If you look directly at them, you can't see them. But if you focus to one side, there they are.

It's never what you think

Please do not misunderstand; along your spiritual path, thinking can help you bridge the gap between moments of awakening. You can use that busy mind to learn through books and tapes, and from time to time you may well have moments of quieting the mind, coming into the present, and experiencing this profound sense of spaciousness, though you may not recognize these moments for what they are. It might feel unfamiliar, perhaps even a little uncomfortable to be so at peace. Why? Because the mind, being what the mind is, says, "Sure, peace is great, but what about opening that checking account?" Learn to trust that profound sense of well-being and presence for more than just a moment or two.

You may not be the best person to judge if you are demonstrating your natural enlightenment. It's something like baking a muddlefrump. How will you know when it is done? How will you know if that's the taste you want? If I had said "baking a chocolate cake," you've all had experiences with chocolate cake. You'd say, "I know chocolate cakes. You bet. I'm a pretty good judge of chocolate cakes."

But what about demonstrating your natural enlightenment? *That* isn't *like* anything else. As students wake up, they regularly have the experience—they regularly get to understand—that *moments of enlightenment are never the same experience twice.* It would make sense, wouldn't it? Because you know what it is to have the same experience over and over and over again. The most difficult part about *not* living a genuinely spiritual life is it just gets boring, it wears you down, and it wears you out.

But in the present, it's never the same experience. That is why a teacher can be entertained by a rose in a vase in a nearly empty room or by a thousand people in a busy shopping mall. He has the opportunity to notice without thinking, without that constant internal chatter like background radiation. It's not there, so he just gets to notice. If you observe him quietly noticing, there's tremendous appreciation being demonstrated. And if you are in his presence, you'll discover yourself being appreciated—or loved—for who you are, exactly as you are.

Epilogue

Between Here and Enlightenment: A Pop Quiz

If you've read this book, I can almost guarantee that you're not a monk sitting in a monastery. But you are almost certainly an above-average, ordinary human being. That's why this book is a guide for the rest of us. I can almost guarantee as well that you're in the middle of a lot of somethings—friends, family, school, work, ambition, health, romance. So what should you do tomorrow about all these somethings?

Take today to reflect on this question—or procrastinate, if you prefer. Then consider the first question in our concluding pop quiz (the "correct" answers follow the quiz). Don't panic; it's a just-for-fun collection of questions and multiple-choice answers, so go ahead and exercise your free will:

The Quiz

Q. How do you keep the hash browns from sticking?

A) Cook expertly.

B) Never turn the stove on.

C) Write your own unique response.

Q. Who cleans up after the horse in overweight horse hockey?

A) Not me.

B) Me—I always do.

C) Choose a response that sounds like someone you may not agree with.

Q. What is the difference between God and Source?

A) Don't ask me, ask God.

B) There is no difference, really.

C) Religious doctrine.

Q. You have five minutes to pray before the end of the world. What do you do?

A) Pause and accept what is.

B) Pray for ten minutes of great sex.

C) Panic creatively.

Q. What's the third dimension?

A) A rock group from the seventies.

B) Depth.

C) The actual world.

Q. What is the IMP?

A) An instantaneous memory of the present.

B) A mischievous being from the netherworld.

C) Write your own response.

Q. Is truth fattening?

A) Yes, because the more you hang on to what you know, the more bloated you get.

B) No, because what is more true for you rather than less true for you has you feel lighter and lighter until you reach enlightenment.

C) All of the above.

The Answers

Q. How do you keep the hash browns from sticking?

A) Cook expertly.

Great answer, but how do you become an expert? Practice, right? And practice is a process of getting better over time. So early on, some of your hash will definitely get scorched.

B) Never turn the stove on.

And you could have added, "leave the potatoes in the bag" or, in our case, in the garden. Do you really think that is possible? If it's not the hash browns, then it will be something else. The metaphor is a good one; it's about timing and distraction as we look to spiritually awaken. You're a human being; you've got to eat, and you're going to get distracted (a lot), but don't let that stop you from making the attempt.

C) Write your own unique response.

If you chose C (and actually wrote a response), you are demonstrating how to generate more possibilities in your life. Don't be intimidated by enlightenment. You are a unique person worthy of your own point of view; in fact, you are worthy of many points of view, evolving and maturing over a lifetime.

Q. Who cleans up after the horse in overweight horse hockey?

A) Not me.

If you've never volunteered to "scoop the poop" after the parade, it would sure seem that it's always someone else's responsibility. Overweight horse hockey is about not noticing what those around you are demonstrating and the mess that creates. If you're still sure that you've never been the one working the shovel, is that because you're the horse?

B) Me—I always do.

I don't believe you. From my perspective, people who are that deliberate about putting themselves in harms way are also actively managing their life situation (even if it is outside their awareness). Look, I'm sure that at times it must feel like you are always on the back end of life. When will you be ready for that to change? Could it be your turn to mount the horse and ride a few laps without obsessing over the consequences?

C) Choose a response that sounds like someone you may not agree with.

As a unique person, you are in fact a collective response of the reactions and opinions of everyone else you have ever met. This doesn't mean you're not important and unique, but it can be very useful to begin to notice those other voices in your head. Sometimes the easiest way to gain a perspective on those influencing you is to not fight with them. Instead, voluntarily and briefly adopt their point of view just to thoroughly appreciate it. That's how you win competence.

Q. What is the difference between God and Source?

A) Don't ask me, ask God.

You are on to something here. While you may address your question to either God or Source, only Source will hear your question. Who answers? God, of course. From my perspective, God is how Source communicates with us. Check out the spiritual literature; from burning bushes to booming voices or a felt presence, when we know God directly it always involves our "senses," especially our "inner senses." It seems that our five senses and their blends are the only ways we have to represent the world to ourselves, and this includes both what appears to be outside of us, inside of us, and greater than us.

B) There is no difference, really; and

C) Religious doctrine.

God and Source are not the same, because Source can never be known. Source could be called the mystery of mysteries, and it has been. I started referring to Source rather than God, because the word "God" has been franchised for so long that it is almost exclusively religious and political. Source can never be defended, explained, codified, or turned into a principle. If that ever happens to the word "Source," then we'll just have to come up with another word.

Q. You have five minutes to pray before the end of the world. What do you do?

A) Pause and accept what is.

Ahhhhh, what a great answer. With that pause comes acceptance. Now you get to say "thank you" and really appreciate everything you have experienced in your brief life—the whole darn setup. Think you could have that much presence of mind if the end came with only five minutes warning? You could if you have practiced a bunch and knew in your bones what it is to enter the present.

B) Pray for ten minutes of great sex.

If you don't know what I'm talking about *and* you're reading this, it's definitely time to talk to your folks. While we're on the subject of sex, do you know that almost every spiritual awakening involves a sexual awakening? This can come as quite a surprise to those who want to escape the body and reside only in the "spiritual." Have I mentioned anywhere in this text that "enlightenment is only for bodies"? Well, it is, and now I've said it.

C) Panic creatively.

Another very interesting answer. Almost anything creative can add a new possibility to your free will. But consider this: enlightenment is not so much a process of addition as it is subtraction, much like a literal death. For many of us, this realization will create a very real panic. Responding from the present in those moments will help alleviate your panic and facilitate your awakening. On the other hand, there will probably be a lot that you will "add" during your life, which could help you to be a more awake, compassionate, and resourceful person—until enlightenment, that is. Then you get to realize that all of it—even the best of it—is just "that which proceeded" waking up in the present forever.

Q. What's the third dimension?

A) A rock group from the Seventies.

Is it? Was it the Third Dimension that recorded "Afternoon Delight"?

B) Depth.

Again, yes it is. Depth is what allows for all this stuff around us to be around us, including ourselves. Depth allows us to "get out of heads" and let Source's set up support us.

C) The actual world.

Again I say, "Yes it is." Well done—three for three. During a public talk on noticing, someone once asked me if what I was talking about (depth) was the natural world. All I could say to her was, "No,

I'm not talking about the natural world, I'm talking about the *actual* world." It is right here, and it has almost nothing to do with the "short hand" we normally experience.

Q. What is the IMP?

A) An instantaneous memory of the present.

Good answer, but how does the IMP influence us? As I write this, I have the impulse not to give you more of an answer than that. Would that offend you or frustrate you if you can't find the answer in the back of the book? Would this bully or *inspire* you to look up IMP and refresh your understanding? I'll support whatever your response is, and remember—those who play are invited to play even more.

B) A mischievous being from the netherworld.

Boy, it sure is, isn't it? If you've happened to take on thoroughly noticing and grasping the IMP at work in life, you know what I mean. Have you heard of the "still, small voice" that is always there to guide us and whose only goal for us is to live in peace at all times? Well, I don't really talk much about "still, small voices," and someday if you want, maybe you'll find a way to ask me why that is. But I understand exactly what this is pointing to—the pause that always precedes creating a *nearly* instantaneous copy of the present. When the IMP lives your life, you can only experience some degree of frustration. If that isn't mischief from the netherworld, I don't know what is.

C) Write your own response.

Sorry, no explanation. Time to make it up for yourself.

Q. Is truth fattening?

A) Yes, because the more you hang on to what you know, the more bloated you get.

Wouldn't that be a hoot—a guide to counting truth calories! So many calories for this thought, so many for that belief, how many hours or lifetimes on average it takes to shed certain principles. Look, I never said that all those thoughts and facts in your life and the world's cultures and history aren't true. Many, if not most, probably are true, but do they lower your blood pressure, help you think more clearly, and guide you to act with more wisdom?

B) No, because what is more true for you rather than less true for you has you feel lighter and lighter until you reach enlightenment.

If out of all these words you can put just this to work in your life, then congratulations. This is how truth can set you free. This is how truth becomes love. The truth that is love cannot divide, or be mean, or cause indigestion. It will appear and inform and nourish you in less than an instant, and then it's gone. Let it go, again and again, until you reside in that place before love and truth were split.

C) All of the above.

Of course it's all of the above, sweetheart; that's how big and compassionate the universe is.

Join in Avocado Consciousness— Play the Book Game

In this special advance edition, we offer you the unique opportunity to take part in the development of books by Steve Whiteman.

Because he resides somewhere in the present, Steve has discovered that he has little to say unless someone asks a question. Much of *Swallowing the Avocado of Enlightenment* comes directly from conversations and dialogues with friends, students, and visitors during public talks, workshops, and retreats. You, too, can take part in the ongoing conversation by playing the Book Game.

All you have to do is respond to the text by asking questions and sharing ideas. If you participate in the Book Game, we will include you in the Acknowledgments of a future edition. After reading the book, send your questions and comments to Trillium Center Press, P.O. Box 1479, Clarkesville, GA 30523, or email stevewhiteman@ alltel.net. Have fun!

If you'd like to order more books, call Trillium Center Press at 888-617-5638, or you can fill out this form and fax it to us at (706) 754-2170, or visit our website to email us and see other products: www.stevewhiteman.com.

QTY	PRODUCT	PRICE	TOTAL
	Swallowing the Avocado of Enlightenment	$22.95	
	Sales Tax: (Georgia residents add 7.0%)		
	Shipping/Handling (Add $4.00 per book)		
	Total		

Call for shipping costs outside the U.S.
Canadian Book Price: $27.95 U.S. · Canadian Shipping: $6.00 U.S.

Shipping Address:

Name

Address 1

Address 2

City   State   Zip/Post Code   Country

Phone   Fax

E-mail

Charge to (Cardholder Name):

Credit Card Number   Expiration Date

Circle One:

Visa   MasterCard   Is this a debit card?   Yes   No

Fax completed order form to: (706)754-2170
If paying by check, mail check and completed form to:
Trillium Center Press
P.O. Box 1479
Clarkesville, GA 30523
Checks payable to Trillium Center Press